Jill Billington

colour your garden

The Royal Horticultural Society

Quadrille

Dedication
To Dawn Farrant, to acknowledge her consummate professionalism
and with thanks for her valued understanding and friendship.

Editorial Director: Jane O'Shea
Creative Director: Mary Evans
Art Director: Françoise Dietrich
Project Editor: Carole McGlynn
Production: Vincent Smith, Tracy Hart
Picture Research: Clare Limpus
Picture Assistant: Samantha Rolfe

Illustrations by Lynne Robinson and Richard Lowther
Special photography by Marianne Majerus

First published in 2002 by Quadrille Publishing Limited
Alhambra House
27–31 Charing Cross Road
London WC2H OLS

This paperback edition first published in 2004

Cataloguing-in-Publication Data: a catalogue record for this book is available
from the British Library.

ISBN 1 84400 079 6

Printed and bound in Singapore

page 1: **The cone-shaped centres of** *Echinacea*
purpurea **are hot orange and gold, in contrast**
to the cool crimson of the encircling petals.

pages 2–3: **The colours in this garden range**
from pale, luminous turquoise seedheads of
Papaver somniferum **to the deep amethyst of**
Eryngium bourgatii. **'Old rose' coloured**
poppies and the wine-pink dots of *Knautia*
macedonica **enrich the cool blue overtones.**

right: **The crimson flowers of** *Rhododendron*
augustinii **subsp.** *augustinii* **have an**
orange throat.

contents

introduction

I have been designing gardens for over twenty-five years and, through my passion for plants, colour has become for me an intriguing and increasingly inspirational part of the garden. Essentially, I feel that my aim as a designer is to create outdoor spaces that have a character or mood that is unique. I invest all my skills as a former sculptor to establish shape and structure that will form the 'bones' of the garden's design, but – probably because it is so emotive – it is always colour that proves to be the most powerful means of establishing atmosphere.

Ideally all gardens should lift the spirits and stir the emotions. And sequences of colour are as mood enhancing as sequences of musical notes, inducing quiet tranquillity, creating energetic vivacity or evoking reassuring warmth. To enjoy plants in a garden means placing them with care, choosing which work well together visually and enhance one another without pointless competition. In this book I try to show how to make gardens or borders in which the chosen colours benefit from their association with others.

right: **Pastel shades associate well, as seen in the harmonious blend of lilac *Verbena bonariensis* with the straw-coloured oaty inflorescences of the grass *Stipa gigantea*.**

Colour is light, and, coming from the north-west of England, with its damp, misty climate, I have been very influenced by the quiet colours of the countryside. Initially my affection for garden colour lay in the soft greens of fields, the lilac-blues of distant hills and the dark green depths of woodland. On the other hand, I have been excited by seeing very different light effects, from the white sunlight of the Mediterranean to the lush, golden brilliance of sub-tropical areas. The colours and, more especially, the plants that hail from these climates are so different and so enticing – would that we could grow them all. However, the restrictions imposed by climate can in fact be a help since any means of aiding decision-making is a gift to the imaginative mind. The blank page, where anything goes, is far more challenging than one where certain rules or restrictions govern the creative process. So an appreciation of different light effects can enable the gardener to master colour rather than the other way round.

In some latitudes colours are seen 'filtered' through blue light and this suggests the use of soft, romantic pastels. On the other hand, brilliant searching sunlight may lead to the choice of strong hues that are not gentled by light but acclaimed by flamboyant association. Not only will the quality of the light affect your attitude to colour but also your experience of placing colours together. No colour is ever seen in isolation, so really 'pure' colour cannot exist in the garden. Today's contemporary elegance demands carefully judged restraint but some prefer the sheer joie de vivre of a multitude of colours. And while the chaos of technicolour is rarely ideal, experiment with contradictory colours can be exciting. In the garden we can derive much pleasure from associating colours, either for harmonious effects or for the challenge of drawing attention to the scene, so that even deliberate discord can be fun – although this should not be merely a matter of throwing any colour into the ring.

I see colour as a celebration of nature as well as an invaluable design tool. I really enjoy colour in a garden, finding in it a key to stimulate the imagination as well as to create atmosphere. My passion for plants encompasses their rich colour diversity, from the subtle shades of small native plants to some of the vibrant new hues wrought by hybridizing. I enjoy tonal contrasts, the use of soft colours in dark situations, even having a fling with brash colours that may not always work. By forming a well-judged harmony, colours may be made to balance each other, to establish rhythms around the garden space and to focus our attention on particular views or a special plant. Above all I like surprises, where everything melds together harmoniously apart from a 'throw' of the unexpected, which prevents the scheme from becoming too safe or somewhat bland.

The artworks that appear throughout the book reveal very different colour effects, which reflect my experience of putting plants together. Whether they are calm and restful or challengingly hot, the illustrated schemes are all based on tried and tested associations or recent, more experimental ideas. Scale is always relevant. Not all gardens are the same size, so some of the planting plans are based on whole gardens, others on parts of gardens, while some depict a simple planting bed. And towards the end of the book I put these schemes in context by referring to specific situations – of climate, sun and shade, and soil – because plants are living things and must be suited if they are to thrive. But even here there is room for experiment and creative opportunities to set up 'foreign' associations in unlikely places.

I hope that by exploring this book readers find some answers but, more importantly, that they gain in confidence when dealing with colour and their imagination is stirred to new endeavours.

left: **Strong sunlight at midday and a cobalt-blue sky overhead provide the right conditions for a Mediterranean-style planting of helichrysum and valerian with other grey-leaved plants.**

exploring colour

introduction

Although the subject of this book is gardening, rather than painting, it is helpful to shed some light on the science of colour and the terms used to describe it. Colour is all-important when making a garden and a skilled selection of plants is the key to a successful planting scheme. For the gardener, then, an understanding of colour is just as useful as an understanding of soil, climate and horticultural procedures.

Each colour has unique properties. It has a 'natural' lightness and darkness: if the full spectrum is photographed using a black-and-white film it will be quite clear that yellow is naturally pale and that purple is the darkest hue. It is obvious, also, that red, orange and yellow are the warm colours of fire and the sun, while the shadows in a glacier are the naturally colder colours, blue and purple. We also notice that colours appear to change in certain lights. Beneath warm yellow electric light, we do not have a true representation of an object's real colour. How often, in a shop, have we had to take something to the window, to see its 'real' colour in daylight? But daylight is not constant, either. The same plant under a leaden sky may look quite drab but as the sun appears the flower colour is enlivened. And when the lights are low, or we are out at dusk, we observe how white and the pale blues leap forward.

There is also a marked variation in our perception of colours in different climates. The light of the Mediterranean and the tropics is searingly bright and the shadows correspondingly laser-sharp and

purpled. These are the geographical areas of extreme colour contrast, which is why colourist painters like Gauguin or van Gogh sought 'the South' for brilliance of colour. It is quite different in the northern latitudes, where the light is softer and slightly bluer: think of Constable oil paintings or the soft English watercolours of Richard Wilson. Paintings from these climates have less startling pure colour and show fewer extremes of light, the colours being reduced in value, with less contrast and often slightly blued in tone.

In most gardens, green will be ever-present. Unlike artists, gardeners are not dealing with a white background; flower colours will usually be seen against foliage, soil or the neutral tones of stone or gravel. And since foliage is constant for much of the year, green can be a real asset, linking or calming all colour schemes.

above: **The soft pink of *Verbascum* 'Helen Johnson' stands out in front of a mass of cool blue centaureas and white centranthus in a cool-climate garden.**

opposite: **A wind-blown garden in Victoria, Vancouver Island, is open to the ocean. It is planted for the sheer enjoyment of flamboyant colour. This sunny garden is filled with scarlet and pink oriental poppies beside lime-yellow euphorbias, pink alpine dianthus, silvery artemisias, scatterings of red valerian (*Centranthus ruber*) and massed golden California poppies (*Eschscholzia californica*), brilliant colours that sit easily in a bright, light-filled space.**

previous page: **Aeonium 'Zwartkop'.**

colour as light

impression of colour. Many surfaces are opaque, making some wavelengths bounce back. A red petal, for example, has absorbed all wavelengths of colour except red. Other surfaces may be described as translucent and light can pass through these after changing its composition in the process.

We know that light travels in straight lines because we cannot see round corners. When it passes through denser material whose surfaces are not parallel, like a glass prism or a raindrop, the rays are bent at an angle with the surface, but because each wavelength bends at a different angle, the light splits into colour. This refracted light creates a spectrum or 'rainbow effect', in which the different wavelengths of colour have separated out.

Each of the spectrum colours has its own wavelength; red is the longest and violet the shortest. As the length of the wave alters the colour changes, gradually assimilating the adjacent hue in the spectrum, so yellow, associating on one side with red, creates orange wavelengths. Its other neighbour is blue, and as yellow begins to mix in,

The science of colour is not exact and we all probably see colours differently, but it helps to pin down what is meant when we talk about colour. The light that reaches us from the sun is made up of radiant energy in a range of wavelengths. If separated, these correspond to the spectrum of colours as seen in the rainbow – the familiar sequence of red, orange, yellow, green, blue, indigo and violet. Alternative light sources, such as light bulbs, usually produce a mixture of wavelengths that are less wide-ranging than those in sunlight. At the extreme, lasers produce light of a single wavelength.

Colour is 'seen' largely by its interaction with surfaces. It is the effect of the surface in selecting or absorbing certain wavelengths that gives the main

with blue, it gradually builds to green that, in its turn, leads to blue. So each colour gradually loses its purity. However, within each colour band there is a central point where the colour, or hue, is untainted by either of its neighbours and is a pure colour. For example, there is a pure yellow that is neither orange-biased nor lime-biased. The pure hues are at the crest of their own special wavelength.

colour theory

Despite our scientific knowledge, colour theory is still open to interpretation, whether devised by painters or scientists. It was Sir Isaac Newton who developed colour theory as a study of the properties of light. He thought that he could clearly observe seven distinct hues when white light is refracted into the spectrum. At one end he 'saw' two distinct colours, namely indigo and violet, which today are more easily linked together as purple. Since seven has been a mystical number throughout history, the theory fitted neatly at the time. After this Goethe wrote his famous 'Theory of Colours' in which he went back to the studies of painters like Leonardo da Vinci and decided that colour was entirely a matter of perception, that is, how the eye sees it.

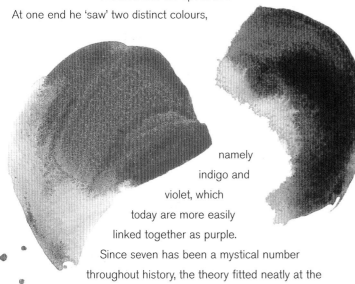

The colour wheel was a convenient invention that has been used for almost three centuries. In it there are three primary colours – red, yellow and blue – from which three secondary colours – orange, green and purple – could be mixed. These colours were twinned with their opposites, or complementaries: red with green, blue with orange and purple with yellow. They were shown to have dramatic effects of contrast, to the point where a pure colour would appear to 'jump' if placed within a mass of its complementary hue. If you stare at a clearly shaped object that is red, then close your eyes, you will then 'see' the same shape in green. Opposite, or complementary, colours were exploited by painters, particularly the Impressionists, who followed this lead by using the complementary colour within the shadow of an object. Claude Monet's paintings of a haystack show his passion for, and his exploration of, colour. Today both the physics of light and the amazing array of paints and dyes now available to artists continue to fascinate us.

It is significant that Gertrude Jekyll was a painter before she became a gardener and she too developed colour theories, this time for garden application. She was much influenced by the colour-wheel theories of Michel Chevreul, an expert in dyes and director of the Gobelin tapestry factory, in early Victorian times. He stated that there were warm colours to one side of the colour wheel, like the red to yellow range, and cool ones on the other side. The warm colours were shown to be dynamic, that is demanding attention, while the cooler colours, being more retiring, were seen as harmonious and unchallenging. But harmonies can also be created by placing together colours that are adjacent in the colour wheel (see Colour as a Design Ingredient, page 82).

the influence of neighbouring colours

Just as colours appear to have a physical effect on us, they also greatly affect each other, since a colour is hardly ever seen on its own. The only way to see a pure hue isolated from others is in the dark, an experience that is highly unlikely. So every hue is viewed as part of a whole range of other colours, shades and tones that are close to it. These surroundings influence the way we see a colour. Sometimes it is enhanced, for example by being closely associated with an adjacent or analogous colour from the spectrum sequence. An example would be yellow and orange next to scarlet, like a mass of wallflowers (*Erysimum cheiri*) in spring. At other times the darkness of one colour reveals more of a lighter one, like the fluffy white flowers shown so well over the deep red-purple foliage of

Cimicifuga simplex 'Brunette' or the pale parchment colour of golden oat grass (*Stipa gigantea*) against the heavy, dark green leaves of *Crambe cordifolia*. Equally, the paleness of a colour makes its associate seem darker as, for example, when surrounding the already intense blue of *Anchusa azurea* 'Loddon Royalist' with pale silvery *Artemisia ludoviciana* 'Valerie Finnis'.

Even monochromatic combinations in the flower border can reveal how a colour is moderated by its neighbour. For example, in a blue border, consider the blue gradually being changed in tone by the addition of red – the border becomes livelier. So a border dominated by large masses of dark and pale blue campanulas, delphiniums, salvias and scabious would be enlivened by light pink flowers, such as those of *Sidalcea* 'Elsie Heugh', the deeper pink spires of *Lythrum virgatum* 'The Rocket' or massed dots of red *Knautia macedonica*. The effect of the pink or red intrusions warms the border slightly and also adds depth to it, because red appears to advance and blue to retire. This is a real asset, without which flower borders can appear decorative but rather flat.

Gertrude Jekyll explored warm and cool colours in composing her borders. Her valuable colour examples can be seen in the plans for the herbaceous borders in her own garden, at Munstead. One border 60m (200ft) long and 12m (40ft) deep develops as a sequential colour scheme with a central 'crescendo' of dynamically associated reds, oranges and yellows. Texture and form are major design tools that further characterize Miss Jekyll's 'pictures'.

opposite above: **In a monochrome association of orange-yellow *Rudbeckia fulgida* var. *sullivantii* 'Goldsturm' with golden *Heliopsis helianthoides* var. *scabra* 'Sommersonne', the yellows are further energized by a contrasting slim band of rich lavender-blue *Aster* x *frikartii* 'Mönch'.**

opposite below: **Being pale versions of the true hues of complementary purple and yellow, the lilac-mauve *Verbena bonariensis* is luminous beside straw-coloured *Stipa gigantea*.**

above left: **Hot orange oriental poppies accentuate the mahogany-red of the neighbouring bearded irises. The intervention of soft pink aquilegia adds subtle contrast.**

above centre: **The orange of the silken petals of California poppies 'jumps' out when placed next to its near-complementary, the deep purple of the prairie gentian (*Eustoma grandiflorum*).**

above right: **Exploiting the tension between warm and cool, the cold magenta *Lychnis coronaria*, further chilled by silver foliage, clashes wonderfully with scarlet *Achillea* 'Fanal', with mustard-centred eyes.**

hue and intensity

Hue means pure colour – like red or blue – neither paled nor darkened, nor contaminated by its adjacent colour in the range of the spectrum. Thus the pure unadulterated hue, for example red, would be described as red but more often it becomes scarlet if it contains some orange, or crimson or wine-red if it includes a greater quantity of blue. Similarly we refer to acid, or lemon, yellows, meaning those on the green side of the pure hue, or use the adjective golden or mustard for those yellows moving towards orange. And blues may be turquoise, if close to green, or indigo when leaning towards purple.

The intensity of a colour lies in its saturation – an intense red implies the pure, undiluted concentration of that hue. At the beginning of the twentieth century Alfred Munsell devised a colour classification system in which he showed that colours could, in effect, be muddied, not necessarily made darker or lighter but less intense, less pure. He described this as the chroma.

Many wildflowers and herbs are simply coloured and for many years were overlooked because gardeners sought more intense, brilliant colour. This is quite clear if we look at the development of hybrid roses, bred to produce amazingly bright colours. *Rosa* Orange Sensation and *R.* Danse du Feu were a great success when they came on to the market because of the intensity of their hue, though it must be said that disease resistance and long flowering made them even more welcome. On the other hand, many 'old' roses, such as *R.* 'Charles de Mills' or the greyed *R.* 'Veilchenblau', were a purpled wine-red, more allied to rubies than to garnets. Today's rose breeders have now returned to the older colours and blended them with the remarkable saturated hues of the more recent past to produce roses in subtle shades of mauve, ruby, old gold and brown.

From the gardener's point of view, flower colours are often muted, less brilliant versions of the parent hue, which is just as well because we do not always want 'jewel' colour. Continuously intense colours would strain the eyes, rather like old-fashioned Technicolor on the cinema screen, while the more muted colours create far more subtle effects. We hardly ever come across absolutely pure saturated colour effects in the plant world, though the flowers of yellow *Achillea filipendulina* 'Gold Plate', red *Crocosmia* 'Lucifer' and blue *Salvia guaranitica* 'Blue Enigma' are all good examples of intense colour. There is greater interest and subtlety in the less saturated colours of newly popular plants like *Verbascum* 'Helen Johnson', described as having 'antique apricot' flowers, or poppies of a soft greyed pink, like *Papaver orientale* 'Patty's Plum'. The blooms of *Penstemon* 'Sour Grapes' are not quite mauve but bluish and the petals of *Rosa* 'Julia's Rose' may best be described as parchment-coloured. Among bearded irises there are some remarkably complex colours as well as very intense ones. For example, *Iris* 'Langport Chapter' is an intensely regal purple, whereas *I.* 'Langport Duchess' has a low-key but exquisite flower, described by the breeder as 'a blend of violet, coffee and bronze with touches of gold in the beard'.

opposite above: **Few red flowers have such saturated colour as *Crocosmia* 'Lucifer'.**

opposite below: **Here, the red of *Crocosmia* 'Lucifer' is perceived as more orange by its close association with saturated yellow *Achillea filipendulina* 'Gold Plate'.**

left: Delphinium **'Blue Nile' is an intense blue.**

with white. So pink *Monarda* 'Beauty of Cobham' would look pleasing alongside *Phlox paniculata* 'Starfire', both being basically 'blue' reds. She had similar favourite schemes in which white was the third, harmonizing party. She often chose to combine pale blue with mid-blue and white, for example by mixing tall masses of white *Gypsophila paniculata* 'Bristol Fairy' with smaller, light lavender-blue *Nepeta racemosa* 'Six Hills Giant' and mid-blue *Veronica austriaca* 'Crater Lake Blue'. Silver foliage was frequently included.

Among the properties of colour there is a 'natural' assumption that yellow is light and purple is dark. So we would expect golden-yellow *Coreopsis grandiflora* 'Mayfield Giant' to be very bright in a border of herbaceous plants and *Aconitum carmichaelii*, with deep blue flowers, to be retiring because it is far darker. But of course there are also dark yellows, verging upon ochre, deep orange and brown, like *Helenium* 'Goldrausch' or the slightly more orange yellows of *Achillea* 'Old Brocade' or *A.* 'Terracotta'. Any of these would be an unusual but effervescent partner with flowers in a pale value of purple, described as lilac, lavender or mauve, such as the fluffy *Thalictrum delavayi* 'Hewitt's Double'. On a smaller scale, consider the exciting effect when the flowers of pale mauve *Viola* 'Inverurie Beauty' or the gloriously lilac-speckled small-flowered *V. sororia* 'Freckles' are seen nestling with the brown foliage of *Carex comans* 'Kuperflamme'.

The value of a colour is simply its brightness, its shade – that is, its darkness or lightness. Colours may be paled into pastel representations of themselves, like cream, powder-blue, lavender, pink, peach, jade or glaucous colours. Or they may be darkened or muddied by the inclusion of other colours, producing ochre, mustard, rust, bronze, chocolate, claret, plum, olive, bottle, Prussian or navy.

A colour may have a high or low value, that is, be a pale or dark shade. *Malva moschata*, with its flowers of pale pink, has a high value, whereas maroon-red *Knautia macedonica* is low in value. Similarly, the luminous pale blue bellflowers of *Campanula persicifolia* 'Telham Beauty' contrast with the low value of the dark purple-blue bells of *C. latifolia* var. *macrantha*. Even within one genus of plants, like lavenders, different varieties may have dark and others pale values. *Lavandula* x *intermedia* Old English Group has light bluish flowers whereas those of *L. angustifolia* 'Hidcote' are dark purple.

Miss Jekyll appears here again. She resolved that pastel colours, those paled by white, look good with their parent colour as well as

opposite: Intense magenta *Lychnis coronaria*, growing from pale grey leaves and branching stems, makes a flagrant display against the backcloth of deep brown-purple *Phormium tenax* 'Nanum Purpureum'. Inset is a dark red form of the annual opium poppy (*Papaver somniferum*), with pale glaucous foliage.

left above: In a luminously pale form of magenta, another opium poppy (*Papaver somniferum* 'Paeony Flowered') rises through waves of the pastel green ornamental grass (*Hordeum jubatum*).

left below: Velvety *Rosa* 'Cardinal de Richelieu' is one of the deepest wine-purple gallica roses.

perceptions of value

As we saw earlier, colour is a matter of individual perception. We assume that we all recognize colours as being the same, but we know that some people are colour blind and confuse colours like red and green or, more rarely, blue and orange. It is possible that even people who are not colour blind do not realize that their perception is less keen than that of others. Certain wavelengths of colour may be less easily absorbed by an individual, just as there are people whose hearing is partial, without being deaf. They may hear the lower pitches normally, or more clearly than the higher ones. In the same way, the subtlety between tones and values of a colour can be difficult to gauge. A colleague at art school had great

difficulty with hue but registered value more easily than many of us because the colour 'did not get in the way'. His still-life paintings were a lesson in light.

Sometimes flower colour can also get in the way of our seeing light and dark values. I often find blue and yellow herbaceous borders unattractive because many of them are planned regardless of colour value and the yellows are as bright as the blues. Where can the eye rest? It is preferable to increase the use of cream, a natural blender, and choose to put in some paler versions of familiar yellows, like *Phlomis russeliana* in place of the more sulphurous *P.* 'Edward Bowles'. This is not to say that strong yellows should be excluded altogether, just that some thought should be given to the

above: **The dark, partially shaded setting is the perfect foil for pale foxgloves, roses and shasta daisies.**

opposite: **Against the dark depths of a yew hedge, light and dark values of blue are fully explored using nepeta, salvias and cornflowers, linked by violet-purple thalictrum and wine-coloured lupins that fuse with the scheme. The border is enlivened by a 'throw' of cold pink tanacetum.**

shade of the flower colour used, so that bold yellows are modified by paler associates. The blues could include some darker forms of flowers too, like deep blue *Geranium* 'Kashmir Purple' as well as pale blue *G. pratense* 'Mrs Kendall Clark'.

We are familiar with the idea of using the shade of colours to set one another off, in the sense that a dark background makes a perfect foil for pale-coloured flowers or leaves. A yew hedge makes the ideal backdrop for herbaceous plants because of its dark, dense foliage and there are other dark-leaved evergreen shrubs that would make a good background hedge. Against such depths, all the white flowers, like shasta daisies (*Leucanthemum* x *superbum* 'Wirral Supreme'), cream *Verbascum* 'Gainsborough', pale pink *Eremurus robustus* or light blue *Delphinium* 'Blue Jade', reveal their shapes well. And silver foliage, like that of the cardoon (*Cynara cardunculus*), tall artemisias and the biennial Scotch thistle (*Onopordum giganteum*), looks magnificent displayed in front of dark foliage.

the garden's depth

The value of a colour has another garden application because dark colours tend to recede and light ones appear closer. If you think of the effect of distance on landscape, not only is everything bluer but all colours also become much paler the further away they are. This characteristic is used to advantage in smaller gardens where the apparent space can be increased by choosing to place dark colours furthest away and paler ones closer to the house. For example, shrubs in the dark red range, like *Cotinus coggygria* 'Royal Purple' and *Sambucus nigra* 'Guincho Purple' will appear further away than shrubs with silver or variegated leaves. One of the brightest is *Elaeagnus angustifolius* 'Quicksilver', another is *Pittosporum tenuifolium* 'Irene Paterson', with its pale mottled jade-green and white leaves. Yellows, too, appear to advance, such as the butter-bright *Philadelphus coronarius* 'Aureus'.

Because light colours appear to expand, a mass of white flowers like ivory *Phlox paniculata* 'Fujiyama' will appear larger than a similarly sized mass of darker flower colours, say, dark purple *P. paniculata* 'Blue Paradise'. This is an important consideration in planning a border; if you want the dark mass to be the main colour, with the lighter shade of flower to be used as incidentals, you will have to plant the darker flowers in larger groups. So all the lighter colours, like yellows and the pastels, will expand and appear larger, in the mass, than their darker counterparts.

As with all aspects of life, fashion plays a part in changing affections. Where once associations of pale silvers and pastels were much prized, now it is the turn of the darker and richer shades.

tone

Tone implies that a colour is warm or cool. To take obvious examples, the flame colours of crocosmia or *Lychnis chalcedonica* are hot and the blues of flowers like anchusa or nepeta appear cool. In winter, when all colour is subdued and most outdoor colour is cold and without a hint of warmth, wearing red is not only cheerful but also appears to notch up the temperature. Conversely, in hot weather, red has far less appeal while blue helps us to cool down. Put together, these two extremes make a complete contrast of tone. Since we perceive each one as an equally strong tonal statement, they are difficult to enjoy together because there is no means of resolving which matters most, and we are left uneasy. In the border, a mass of scarlet monardas beside a similarly sized mass of blue salvias would seem uninteresting, neither one catching the attention, and we might search elsewhere for a place to rest the eye. What would make red and blue work together when the former leans towards warmth and the latter is distinctly cooler?

By appreciating that there are tonal gradations in colour it is possible to link hues for harmonious effect by staying within the hot or cool theme. And any hue can actually belong to either group, depending on how much of its opposite is mixed with the parent colour. So even though we associate red with the hot colour schemes, it can fit into a cool plan if it is crimson, carmine, claret, cerise or a cold bluish pink. Mix these colours with blues that are just slightly warmed with red – that is, royal blue and indigo – and, here again, the paler values like mauve would slide in nicely without upsetting the apple cart. In planting terms these cooler reds could include red valerian (*Centranthus ruber*), *Achillea* 'Cerise Queen', *Hemerocallis* 'Summer Wine', *Echinacea purpurea*, *Penstemon* 'Garnet' and pink sidalcea, as well as the many cold pinks in the geranium family, like the small lilac-pink *Geranium cinereum* 'Ballerina'.

The tones for a hot red scheme would include scarlet, rust, copper, terracotta, and red to orange. Appropriate flower colour could be found among herbaceous plants such as *Achillea* 'Feuerland', *Hemerocallis* 'Chicago Fire', coppery heleniums, *Geum* 'Red Wings', *Heuchera* 'Red Spangles' and *Astilbe* 'Fanal'.

right: The raspberry-pink fluffy flowerheads of *Sedum spectabile* 'Brilliant' are warmed by the orange chrysanthemum in the foreground.

handling tone

It is a worthwhile exercise to take one colour and consider it from a tonal point of view. Yellow is an interesting colour because it is also the trickiest to handle in the garden. We associate it with sunlight and perceive it as warm: buttercups and sunflowers, those sunny chrome-yellows, leap to mind. These central yellow hues need only a little scarlet in them to tip the balance towards colours like peach or apricot, or even ginger. So a range of yellows suited to the warm-toned border might include *Achillea* 'Coronation Gold', *A.* 'Marmalade', *Hemerocallis* 'Berlin Yellow', *H.* 'Golden Prize' and *Geum* 'Lady Stratheden' as well as solidago, inulas and rudbeckias.

But there are yellows that are more allied to the moon than to the sun. Think of cool lemony or acidic tones like those of *Achillea* 'Taygetea', *Anthemis tinctoria* 'E.C. Buxton' and *Coreopsis verticillata* 'Moonbeam'. The lime-green flowers of euphorbias like *Euphorbia characias* subsp. *wulfenii*, or the brassy yellow of *E. polychroma*, do not fit in easily, being sharp or slightly murky and certainly cool toned. Yet the warm tones of *E. griffithii* 'Dixter' or the similar 'Fireglow' are brick-orange, so they belong readily in a warm-toned scheme. The lime-yellows do not look good with the warm ones and a plan can be ruined by linking, say, *Lonicera nitida* 'Baggesen's Gold' with primrose-yellows. These tonal yellows come from different stables and can only mix if one is very pale.

Some ochre-yellows, even further removed from saturated yellow, edge towards brown, which has become a fashionable colour for gardens. Brown foliage is sought out in bronze fennel, brown sedges like *Carex comans* and 'brown' euphorbias, like *Euphorbia dulcis* 'Chameleon', which are all warm-toned. They are quite different from the cooler tones of deep red foliage like orach or red-leaved heucheras, both of which have blue-grey overtones.

The basis of yellow alters in intensity, value and tone as it leans towards adjacent green, orange or red.

top row, from left:
- **Osteospermum 'African Summer'** in front of ***Argyranthemum frutescens***
- **Oenothera biennis** ● **Achillea 'Walther Funcke'**

second row, from left:
- **Nicotiana alata** with **Limonium sinuatum**
- **Narcissus 'Pinza'** ● **Stipa gigantea** seen through **Verbena bonariensis**

third row, from left:
- **Carex elata 'Bowles' Golden'** among leaves of **Alchemilla mollis**
- **Dahlia 'Moonfire'** with **Verbena 'Quartz Scarlet'** against **Salvia microphylla**
- **Larix decidua**, red **Acer palmatum 'Fireglow'**, orange **A. palmatum 'Tsukumo'**

bottom row, from left:
- **Anthemis tinctoria 'Sauce Hollandaise'** ● **Kniphofia 'Bees Sunset'**
- **mixed tones in a 'Cretan meadow' planting**

subjective response to colour

Deep down, we all have an individual preference for certain colours. The natural light of our climate as well as an individual's own 'colouring' tend to influence our colour choices, either consciously or unconsciously. On the whole those with pale skin colouring cannot wear lime or orange, because these colours, neither dark nor light, are also totally without the bluish overtones of a fair skin. Yet on a dark skin such colours are dramatic and exciting. Perhaps our preference for certain colours is governed by the setting that suits each one of us, narrowing the choice down to the colours among which we feel happiest.

Because colour is emotive, it can be chosen, for example when painting a room, to influence a person's mood or even moderate a natural disposition. A look around the home we live in reveals whether we prefer neutral colours, a dramatic background or we need to surround ourselves with a harmonious scheme. Some rooms are cool and almost colourless, suggesting that space, form and texture are more important to the owner and control and organization the means of expression. Other interiors are warm, friendly and inviting, filled with rich detailed contrasts of colours that excite one another. As a garden designer I always discuss the interior with a client because we both discover what colours please and will continue to give pleasure outdoors. Sometimes a contrast is wanted, such as a blaze of yellow outside a white room, or refreshing greens seen through the window of a high-tech steel kitchen. But most people prefer to harmonize interior colours with garden colour, linking indoors with outside.

The garden, then, may both reflect a person's temperament and satisfy a deeply felt need. A majority of gardeners want their personal space to be tranquil, with many greens, blues, pastels and silver foliage plants. Those with an exhausting working life or an excitable disposition, especially, derive comfort from such cool unchallenging hues. But harmony is not the key for everyone and others revel in challenge and want a more experimental colour scheme. This might be a capricious assortment of clashing colours like pink and magenta with lime, gold and rusty orange. Others simply enjoy the revitalizing effect of bold, strong hues and

contrasts of value, so crimsons flash with purples, yellow ignites orange and dark foliage sets off butter-yellow or luminous lilac hues.

We do not necessarily stay loyal to our preferences, however. Some years ago I developed a passion for rust-reds with browns, golds and deep purpled blues. Today I almost need the mix of greens found in damp temperate countryside with shades of cream and deep blue-green woodland colours. We all change over time as experience alters us and makes new approaches relevant. Fashion too affects how we react to colour combinations. There was a time, in the late nineteenth century, when green with blue was considered vulgar. Today this seems absurd. The sky is blue and most of the countryside green so there is no sense in which we can find these two colours incompatible.

Another momentous change in our attitude to colour came at the start of the twentieth century as a result of the great Henri Matisse and Les Fauves school of painting. It was these painters who espoused the cause of 'barbaric' colour and 'violent harmonies', having looked at conventional harmonies and found them wanting. Enabled by more and better paints, they clashed red with pink and orange with bright yellow, creating rich scenes that demanded attention and made new colour relationships acceptable. This approach has filtered down into everyday use and been very influential. Today the use of racy clashing colours can be seen in gardens and has made the 'exotic' garden style fashionable.

Despite our personal colour preferences, there is a level on which people in all cultures find meaning in colour and respond emotionally to it. Even though the symbolic use of different colours varies across continents and even countries, the emotional response is universal. Bright red is always a dynamic and vivid experience, yellow is cheerful and blue calms the mood. We shall look briefly at the different hues to see how this finds expression in the garden.

red

Primary red is the most dynamic of all the colours; it warms us physically and energizes us psychologically. Used everywhere as the signal for danger, red is a colour that demands a response and arouses us from passivity. It is one of the extrovert colours, the 'life and soul of the party' colours, the restless, active hues. The colour of flames in the fire, red also conveys reassuring warmth. Fast food restaurants are often dominated by reds and oranges, not only as an invitation to indulge but also designed to speed us on our way.

In the garden, the reds are dramatic and unmissable. Flowers in hot, exciting colours can blend reds together, riveting attention in early to midsummer. In a sunny border, consider plants such as tall scarlet *Papaver orientale* 'Turkenlouis', *Hemerocallis* 'Canadian Goose', a brilliant red daylily with a yellow throat, fiery *Crocosmia* 'Lucifer' and the giant red hot poker, *Kniphofia* 'Prince Igor'.

Pink originates in red but this colour appeals to those who are less driven or excitable than the red fanciers. Pink is a romantic colour, with great charm, and is the basis of many classic romantic gardens. Early in the season we may use pretty dicentras like *Dicentra* 'Stuart Boothman' in low masses at the front of a bed, its pink flowers reaching delicately above grey-green feathery foliage. Diascias, which last through summer, may be cool ice-cream pinks, such as *Diascia rigescens* or *D. vigilis*, while others, like *D.* 'Ruby Field', are more salmon-coloured, a tone that does not fit nearly as well into a cool pink scheme. The clear pink *Geranium endressii* flowers all summer as does the taller *Lythrum virgatum* 'The Rocket', with deeper pink flower spires. The sharper pink flowerheads of *Achillea* 'Forncett Candy' have a mauve overtone while the pink of *Monarda* 'Beauty of Cobham' is toned down almost to lilac by the purplish calyces around the base of the flower.

yellow

Yellow, the primary colour associated with sunlight, implies optimism and good cheer. Many warm yellow herbaceous perennials are powerfully effective in the mass, like long-lasting rudbeckias such as *Rudbeckia fulgida* 'Goldsturm' and late-season heliopsis. But I feel that the overuse, or mixing, of some yellows can be agitating, so care is needed when placing them (see page 28). You will hear the phrase 'sickly yellow' used on occasion, and in the garden context such unpleasing relationships can occur when, for example, the cool canary-yellow of *Robinia pseudoacacia* 'Frisia' is underplanted with orange-yellow foliage, as of *Spiraea bumalda* 'Goldflame'.

Among the welcoming yellows of spring are narcissi in their huge numbers of varieties. The naturalized daffodils that sweep the fields in the English Lake District, commemorated by the poet Wordsworth, are the loveliest, most closely resembled by *Narcissus*

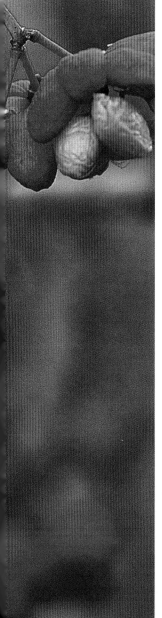

left: **Nature got there before Matisse. Fuchsia-pink seed capsules clash with the hot-coloured orange fruits of *Euonymus europaeus* 'Red Cascade'.**

right: **Orange, red and yellow candelabra flowers of *Primula bulleyana* are a heart-warming sight in spring in a damp area. Behind are stately cream flowers of *Zantedeschia aethiopica*.**

'W.P. Milner'. The elegant, small early-flowering *N.* 'February Gold' is a deservedly popular form, while the tiny narcissi, like forms of *N. cyclameneus* and *N. bulbocodium*, have great appeal in scree or courtyard gardens on a really small scale. A few daffodils veer towards orange in colour, while others are cream. There are many other fresh spring yellows like sun-loving crocuses, winter aconites (*Eranthis hyemalis*), that carpet bare earth or gravel, and shade-loving erythroniums, such as *Erythronium* 'Pagoda'. Yellow spring bulbs are traditionally associated with spring blues, like chionodoxa, scillas and *Anemone blanda*, but they need not be planted together.

orange

Orange, a secondary colour derived from mixing red with yellow, is less charged and more friendly than yellow. It is a lively colour but can be rather sharp, so in the garden it is best set off by browns or connected to reds, which manage its effervescence. Orange can also be toned with gold to make it more companionable. Think of the heleniums, like *Helenium* 'Coppelia', with its velvety-copper rays of petals and brown eye, and the spreading tawny-orange *Hemerocallis fulva* 'Europa', perhaps overseen by the reddening-orange foliage of the small tree *Sorbus sargentiana*. Oranges like this can thrill, but to make them glow with neon brilliance you need to set them among deep purple, for a real contrast of tone.

Brown can be loosely called an extension of orange. The red-bronze *C.* 'Bronze Elegance', as well as the cream-tipped flower column of *Kniphofia* 'Toffee Nosed'. Consider too the brown foliage of *Physocarpus opulifolius* 'Diabolo' and the herbaceous *Eupatorium rugosum* 'Chocolate', which has maroon-brown leaves.

blue

Blue, the third primary colour, is considered a source of mental relaxation as well as a pacifying colour. For many people, tranquillity is one of the most important attributes of a garden, particularly in today's challenging world. The deep blues tend to imply order and control, hence it is the colour used for organizations, from the police force to airlines. The real asset of blues is that they are so accommodating in the garden, fitting in with many colour schemes.

*opposite: **Iris versicolor 'Thomas' Variety'** makes a purple symphony with the equally damp-loving, magenta **Geranium palustre**.*

*left: **As the substance of the garden, green is sometimes undervalued. Here textures in green include the annual grass Hordeum jubatum, lime-green Nicotiana alata, blue-green palmate-leaved Macleaya cordata and, in the centre, a cabbage that has bolted.***

They cool reds without confronting them and blend with yellows, flattering their brilliance. But sadness is also associated with 'the blues' and blue borders can be rather dour, so use all shades and tones – the powder-blues, the mid- and deep blues, as well as

browns, yellow-browns, blue-browns and those with a purple overtone are most prominent in foliage. Any foliage described as 'purpurea' is likely to be brown rather than purple but it will usually have a dark reddish note. These leaves are useful with orange effects and fun with blues. The power of brown lies in its stability.

Both brown and its pale variants, the beige or parchment colours, have become increasingly fashionable and plant breeders are continually working on new cultivars in this colour range. Look out for the flower colours of *Chrysanthemum* 'Brennpunkt', or lighter

pale lavenders. Most of these can be found in salvias, geraniums and delphiniums. *Salvia* x *sylvestris* 'Mainacht' is a neat plant with tall indigo spires whose effect would be intensified by the deeply violet-blue *Geranium ibericum* or lightened by the mid-blue *G.* 'Rozanne'. Towering above these, a mixed group of hybrid delphiniums might include *Delphinium* 'Blue Tit', another indigo, and the sky-blue *D.* 'Skyline'. Avoid the more mauve delphinium cultivars here, like *D.* 'Ruby' or *D.* 'Turkish Delight' or any pale blues that may be slightly greyish, because they do not enhance blues.

green

Green, a secondary colour mixed from blue and yellow, is the universal colour of gardens and has a unifying effect. All the greens are seen as reliable, whether dark or light, bluish or lime-toned. Even when the power of green is reduced, for example by variegation, by autumnal change, by leaning towards yellow or being coated by a silvery-grey surface, green leaves are a permanent part of the colour scene. The idea of an all-green border may be fun but can actually be rather dull, since texture and form can only do so much. Varying the values of green leaves, from dark to pale, helps as does the inclusion of some green flowers, like those of early euphorbias and hellebores, heucheras and grasses. For summer consider *Kniphofia* 'Forncett Harvest', a tall spire with a touch of yellow, or the taller, lime-yellow *K.* 'Percy's Pride'.

Otherwise, with green, consider the addition of cream flowers, like those of the tried and trusted shrub *Potentilla fruticosa* 'Primrose Beauty' or the smaller *Santolina chamaecyparissus* 'Lemon Queen', with fine emerald-green foliage. For early summer you might use lemon-flowered *Coreopsis verticillata* 'Moonbeam' and, if the soil were rich and damp, light yellow *Thalictrum lucidum* would be wonderfully compatible in a green border.

purple

Purple, the last hue in the spectrum and a mix of red and blue, is seen as the colour of highly creative and perceptive people. The paler violet is associated with antiseptic properties but in the garden there are more romantic associations. Think of lavender, present in all romantic styles of garden, traditional and modern. Purple has a strong emotive effect on a border in that it calms down excitable red and gives it some gravitas. But it will also add sparkle to a yellow-based or orange border because it is the contrasting hue.

In its lighter value – violet or mauve – purple will intensify the naturally retiring powder-blues. Biennial clary (*Salvia sclarea*) adds an almost insubstantial quality that 'lifts' the colours of a summer border. In a similar vein, tall *Penstemon* 'Stapleford Gem' is a summer-long perennial with pale purple-mauve flowers and *Perovskia* 'Blue Spire' has airy flowers of a similar colour produced in late summer.

In its darker shades, purple veers towards black and is the darkest colour you will find in a garden. For the blacker purples, consider inky iris hybrids, such as *Iris* 'Black Swan', and aconites like *Aconitum henryi* 'Spark's Variety', with its dark, hooded flowers.

serendipity

In the context of the whole garden, nature has a massive and humbling input and time can change everything. No matter how planned the garden may be, it is nature as co-designer that increasingly dictates the look of the garden as time passes. Plants grow wider, taller, fuller and the bulk of colour increases or decreases according to the plants' vigour. You have only to look back at photographs taken a few years earlier to see that your garden has completely changed its emphasis and that one block of colour has become subordinate to the spread of another. For example, a slow-growing plant like a magnolia takes time to establish roots and may not flower for five or six years, whereas some strongly coloured flowering shrubs, like the brooms (*Cytisus* varieties), give short-lived pleasure for a few years. But we can to an extent manipulate the effect of time and adjust to the changes.

Of all the garden components, colour is the most transient. The changes of light throughout the day, the week or the time of year will affect its appearance. See the garden change as evening light emphasizes the whites, creams, yellows, lilacs and pale blues, while the reds and purples vanish.

Happily, gardening is not a static form of creativity so it continually rewards the gardener. I value the accidents of nature because they stir the imagination and add a new dimension to an ever-changing garden. Over the last few years, seed from the bulb *Nectaroscordum siculum* has leapt from the hidden 'wilder' part of my garden to appear in quantity among the more organized herbaceous areas. Being quietly coloured, with green-and-maroon pendulous umbels, it has fitted in easily so will be allowed to stay and multiply. But the equally prolific lemon-yellow evening primrose (*Oenothera biennis*) strikes a jarring note where it has seeded, so it will be removed. As new seedlings appear, or the habit of a plant matures quite differently from what was anticipated, recognize these as revitalizing contributions. If they work, hold on to them but if they jar, simply pull them up.

The ultimate in serendipity is the wild meadow garden. Nature is the boss but the farmer has acted as foreman for centuries,

above: **The Himalayan blue poppy, *Meconopsis grandis*, is a vivid blue, tamed here within a triangle of equally brilliant contrasting orange-flowered roses, geums and poppies. Two different lime-green euphorbias add another striking colour note. At the back bronze fennel, purple alliums and deep indigo irises provide the dark foil that makes the scheme successful.**

allowing cows into the fields to 'mow' the grass at just the right time to produce either spring- or summer-flowering meadows. The type of soil determines which plants are successful but most soils produce a rich range of colour from native wildflowers, including the pale lime-green mignonette (*Reseda lutea*) to the bright scarlet field poppies (*Papaver rhoeas*). Factors like the fertility, acidity, dryness or dampness of the soil will change plant communities, thereby altering their colours. But the most beautiful characteristic of a meadow is the way all the flowers are displayed against a wispy backcloth of intermingling green-textured grasses and sedges.

In a flowering meadow, some wildflowers do better than others, gradually changing the colour balance. White ox-eye daisies (*Leucanthemum vulgare*) and the flat white flowerheads of yarrow (*Achillea millefolium*), for example, will always create dense patches of one colour. Many other flowers tend to be scattered randomly as

repeating dots of colour, like golden meadow buttercups (*Ranunculus acris*) and yellow dandelions (*Taraxacum officinale*), which appear everywhere. Concentrations of purple knapweed (*Centaurea nigra*) or masses of mauve-blue cranesbills (*Geranium pratense*) always stand out, while the 'plates' of pale blue field scabious (*Knautia arvensis*) are smaller, their subtle beauty more easily seen at close quarters.

above: **A collection of South African plants in a wildflower garden creates a mingling, self-seeding meadow tapestry. Tall kniphofias, watsonias and arching dieramas rise from seas of daisy flowers – Livingstone daisies, ursinias and osteospermums. Yellow and orange poppies add brilliance. Such superb 'managed chaos' must always be a part of gardening.**

the mood of the garden

The garden scene may be 'composed' through the use of colour much as the composer orchestrates notes to make music. The details, in the form of individual plants, build up to create the whole production and set the mood, or tenor, of the garden. Like a musical score, there will be high points that dominate, set against quieter and slower 'passages' of colour that unite the piece. Not all the colours in the chorus would be noticed at first glance, since the role of many of the selected colours is to be a foil. But a second level of interest should be observed after a while: not a background but a rhythmical linking of colours that echo around the garden space.

The tranquil scene would have nothing that jars, so harmonious colours – those close to one another in the spectrum – are blended. This is quite different from the vibrant garden in which colour is chosen for gaiety, hues are those high in value, bright and full of contrast. Neither scheme suits the more natural approach, popular today, in which colours are less those of hybridized luxury or boldly hued exotics but are closer to the tints of nature. As a complete contrast, colours that fit with the chic image of contemporary gardens are carefully selected and controlled.

a note on growing conditions

While designing with colour may be the foundation of this book, it is important that the conditions of the site or the soil are suitable for the chosen plants or they will not grow well. Avoid the risk of such disappointment by being sure that you have the right condition of sun or shade, suitable soil and enough space for the plant's width and height. In the text I make it clear where there is a specific need, for example if a plant cannot live in chalky or limy soil. Where I suggest tender plants, a sheltered site may be sufficient but your local weather and climatic zone are the best indicator of a plant's suitability. If a plant requires well-drained soil, this may mean that heavy clay has to be well dug, incorporating well-rotted compost and possibly sharp grit to improve its drainage. In sandy soils the addition of garden compost or other bulky organic material will help to retain moisture and nutrition. Where plants prefer damp conditions the text will remind you of this.

left: **Subtle gradations of tone are at work, making light orange *Achillea* 'Marmalade' a perfect companion to level the strident orange verticals of *Alstroemeria aurea* 'Dover Orange'. Scarlet *Lychnis* x *arkwrightii* and purple-red annual orach (*Atriplex hortensis* 'Rubra') add piquancy.**

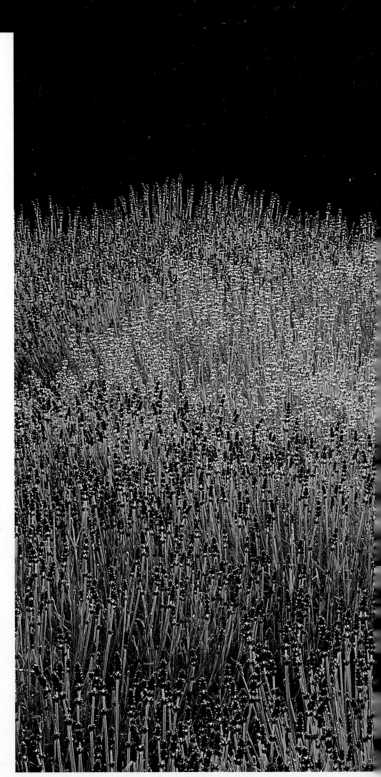

a mood of calm

There are two closely associated colours that are generally acknowledged to restore body and soul, establishing a calm atmosphere in a garden that is soothing to come home to. These are green and blue. Green is seen as the comforting background of life. A verdant garden, with all shades and mixes of green, invites us to take a pleasant stroll through it. Almost everybody likes blue, the colour of the sky. Together, these hues may be used to create a tranquil atmosphere in gardens which are often at their best in spring.

The aim here is to avoid contrast and plan soft shades and harmonies that are undemanding. Provided green is the backcloth, blues of every shade and tone can be chosen. To one side of blue in the spectrum is cobalt, which gradually warms to become midnight, then indigo, heliotrope, purple and ultimately crimson. On the other side of cobalt, Prussian blue merges with turquoise blue and ultimately green and on to lime-green, towards yellow. The two extremities, crimson and lime, may be introduced into a scheme of calm colouring but only in very small quantities. Therefore wine-red knautias or lime-green euphorbias may have only a restricted presence, otherwise they would quickly dominate. The crimson, being warmer, stands out while the lime-green, being brighter, advances. The contemplative blues must set the mood and the incidentals be very subtle.

Always bear in mind plant form, the shape and size of the foliage and the textures on offer. Avoid overdoing the same shape; for example, plants that are spiky, like kniphofias or veronicastrums, are dominant compared with the horizontal layered look of achilleas or phlomis. The same applies with colour: too much contrast should be avoided if you are aiming for a mood of calm, so massed green foliage, like that of thalictrums or anthemis, is ideally neutral.

A MOOD OF CALM **43**

evergreen boundaries

In planning a border, consider first the evergreen backing. Green, permanent boundaries provide a shield against the outside world while also reminding us of nature. This boundary can explore a range of green textures and gentle flowering in different seasons. Evergreens may be dark or light, warm or cold: the greens range from emerald-green laurels to dark, bottle-green yew. Portuguese laurel (*Prunus lusitanica*), a dark-leaved shrub that flatters pale tones in front of it, combines dark formality with a light-reflecting quality.

flowering evergreen shrubs

Where possible, choose shrubs that offer something other than their foliage. Portuguese laurel has ascending candles of white flowers, a further attraction in spring, and there are other shrubs with white or pale flowers that are restful in character. *Osmanthus* x *burkwoodii* has white scented spring flowers and the escallonias flower in summer. *Escallonia* 'Slieve Donard' has very pale pink flowers in summer among densely packed glossy green foliage. My favourite escallonia, *E.* 'Iveyi', has larger leaves and produces panicles of white flowers later in summer. Both these shrubs, particularly the latter, need a warm protected site.

The powder-blue flowers of *Ceanothus* 'Cascade', 4m (12ft) high and wide, trail slightly from this rather lax but charming evergreen shrub in late spring. If your site is protected, consider myrtle, aromatic *Myrtus communis* 'Tarentina' with pretty tufted white flowers that last from midsummer to early autumn. Also for scent, add a rosemary, like *Rosmarinus officinalis* 'Benenden Blue', a clear blue flowering shrub 1.5m (5ft) high and wide. For the smaller garden, *Choisya* 'Aztec Pearl' is hard to beat, with heavily scented white flowers twice a summer and year-round glossy foliage. Always bear in mind that shrubs can grow as tall as small trees in a period of ten to twenty years, so allow for this or prune with care.

There are many other flowering evergreens that help to foster a tranquil blue theme, but I shall limit myself to two specials. For late spring consider the tall, arching, white-flowered *Drimys winteri* for its quite outstanding scented ivory flowers, although it is for acid soils only. For late summer, try the grey-green *Bupleurum fruticosum* with its lime-green flower umbels. Both have special cultural needs, being frost-tender and thriving in the protection of a warm wall.

If a fence or wall backs the borders, evergreen wall shrubs or climbers make a good enclosure, adding to the sense of seclusion. There are several evergreen clematis of which the pale cream-

flowered, fern-leaved *Clematis cirrhosa* 'Wisley Cream' is outstanding because its pretty, pendent cup-shaped flowers appear in winter. On the other hand, frost-hardy *Trachelospermum jasminoides* flowers in mid- to late summer and, as its name suggests, is highly fragrant, carrying terminal racemes of creamy-white flowers. Both evergreen climbers must have support wires or grow through a sturdy tree.

structural shrubs

Having established the permanent backcloth, choose some deciduous shrubs to provide structure and foster a spirit of tranquillity. Most shrubs that flower early in the year have white or yellow flowers, like mahonias and viburnums. White *Chaenomeles speciosa* 'Nivalis' is hardy and has an elegant habit against a wall if pruned sympathetically.

Perhaps you could include a sensuous mauve or pink daphne, or a small lilac, to fill the garden with spring fragrance. Patience is needed, as both are slow growing. *Daphne* x *burkwoodii* 'Somerset', a shrub 1.5m (5ft) high, has soft mauve flowers in late spring, similar in colour to the lilac-coloured *Syringa pubescens* subsp. *patula* 'Miss Kim', a mound growing to 1.8m (6ft) tall, whose flowers gradually fade to blue. The dusty-blue *Ceanothus* 'Gloire de Versailles', only 1.5m (5ft) high and wide, is a fine plant because it has a long-flowering summer season. Later in the season, maintain soft blue colours with a low mound of *Hydrangea macrophylla* 'Blue Wave', about 1.5m (5ft) high, or the slimmer *Hibiscus syriacus* 'Blue Bird', at twice the height. All are suitable for the smaller garden.

For larger gardens the small tree-sized lilac *Syringa vulgaris* 'Mme Lemoine' has bridal white, fragrant flowers in spring. And the horizontally layered *Viburnum plicatum* 'Mariesii', a large shrub wider than it is tall, has a white lace-like quality when in flower in early summer, seen from a distance.

opposite: **Green foliage textures provide a peaceful backcloth for a colour association of purple *Salvia nemorosa* 'Ostfriesland', light blue *Aster frikartii* 'Mönch' and cool magenta *Geranium psilostemon*. Interludes of yellow daylilies and phlomis prevent the scene from becoming bland.**

below: **A sense of tranquillity is fostered by seeing the powder-blue lacecap flowerheads on the low shrub *Hydrangea macrophylla* 'Blue Wave' through the elegant arching stems of the wandflower (*Dierama pulcherrimum*), with its cool, raspberry-pink pendulous flowers.**

CALM BLUE BORDER

A garden full of blue flowers sets the mood early in the year. At the back is the evergreen *Ceanothus arboreus* 'Trewithen Blue', dotted with mid-blue flowers, and beside it a columnar rosemary and the tall, herbaceous *Thalictrum rochebruneanum*, its lilac-blue flowers carried aloft among blue-grey leaves. On the other side a small lilac (*Syringa* 'Miss Kim'), echoes the thalictrum with mauve-blue flower pyramids. Beneath its canopy is a carpet of *Brunnera macrophylla* with sprays of sky-blue flowers, while across the border similar flower sprays of deeper azure-blue belong to *Omphalodes verna*. Early-flowering perennials include tall *Anchusa azurea* 'Loddon Royalist' and clumps of china-blue *Iris sibirica* 'Flight of Butterflies' with emerald-green grass-like foliage. The border is edged with geraniums and *Viola sororia* 'Freckles', with speckled hyacinth-blue flowers. Injecting a little vitality are *Dicentra spectabilis* 'Alba' creamy spires of *Aconitum* 'Ivorine' and lemon-yellow daylilies. Other contrasts include the knife-like fans of *Iris pallida* 'Variegata', with dove-grey and white sharply cut leaves and violet-blue flowers and the magenta lily-flowered *Tulipa* 'Burgundy'.

herbaceous infill

While trees and shrubs establish the framework, it is herbaceous perennials that pick up the baton to make a garden of quiet colour. In the garden, blue merges with other colours and rarely dominates, with the exception of the electric-blue of some hybrid delphiniums. The darker blues settle into the background and the paler ones never jump forward in the same way as yellow or red. The only time blue really focuses our attention is when the ultra-violet light of evening picks up the violet in many blues and adds an almost fluorescent note. This is not evident at midday.

below: **The freshness of late spring is captured perfectly in lightly shaded woodland. Hosta foliage provides greens of all shades as well as soft lilac-blue flowers.**

from spring to summer

Gentle blues merge particularly well with cream and green and natural combinations of these colours occur in semi-shade. Typical woodland plants include pale-flowered perennials such as hellebores, pulmonarias, epimediums, brunneras, anemones, lily of the valley, ferns and acid-loving creamy smilacina (these are described on page 160).

At the edge of a lightly shaded area, geraniums are invaluable. Among them are several delicate, unchallenging light blues like *Geranium pratense* 'Mrs Kendall Clark', with luminous pale blue flowers. The shorter *G. himalayense* 'Irish Blue' would add a slightly deeper colour, although it does spread. So does *G. wallichianum* 'Buxton's Variety', a striking sky-blue without any mauve tint, that in late summer meanders around all other plants. A recent introduction, *G.* 'Rozanne' is a two-toned blue with violet overtones.

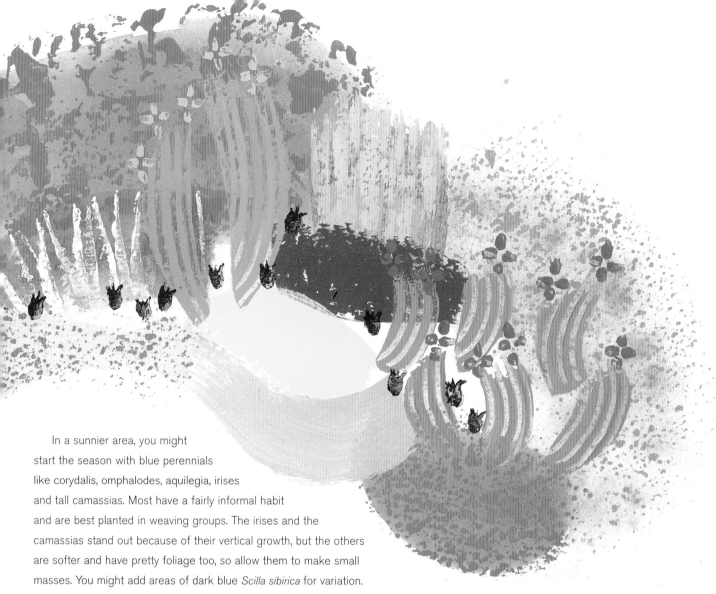

In a sunnier area, you might start the season with blue perennials like corydalis, omphalodes, aquilegia, irises and tall camassias. Most have a fairly informal habit and are best planted in weaving groups. The irises and the camassias stand out because of their vertical growth, but the others are softer and have pretty foliage too, so allow them to make small masses. You might add areas of dark blue *Scilla sibirica* for variation.

As summer comes, the calm garden becomes dependent on the subtleties of cooling blues. Some geraniums will flower in summer heat and other herbaceous perennials, like delphiniums, lupins, irises, scabious and frothy nepeta, work effectively as gentle statements. Try some of the following plants in combination. Create a platoon of green-flowered *Kniphofia* 'Green Jade' with flower spikes of 1.2m (4ft) and add in a few *Echinops ritro* 'Veitch's Blue', with intensely blue drumstick flowers. You might soften these with contrast groups like *Iris sibirica* 'Flight of Butterflies', a pale blue iris 75cm (2ft 6in) high, or the smaller, darker *I. sibirica* 'Baby Blue'.

A cluster of *Sisyrinchium striatum* would bring a crisply defined outline, its slender spikes of cream flowers rising from grey-green iris-like leaves. Behind them you might group a softer background of *Thalictrum delavayi* 'Hewitt's Double', a fluffy pompon-flowered mauve-blue plant 1.2m by 60cm (4ft by 2ft). *Anthemis tinctoria* 'Sauce Hollandaise', covered with cream daisies, could front the group, at 60cm (2ft) high. If there is room you might fit in some groups of scabious, like *Scabiosa caucasica* 'Clive Greaves', an old form with small tufted plates of lavender-blue flowers held aloft for

several weeks. I have a penchant for the neat pale blue *Campanula persicifolia* 'Telham Beauty', an ideal flower for smaller gardens that can easily be inserted among other perennials, weaving through them as a thin blue line of nodding powder-blue flowers.

from summer to late summer

The classic blue perennials, such as delphiniums and lupins, will have finished flowering soon after midsummer, so to sustain this mood of calm into the second half of summer you must rely on other plants.

Provided the site is sunny and sheltered, you could add a splendid late-year injection of *Galtonia viridiflora*, with 60cm (2ft) spires holding nodding green-skirted bells, accompanied by the intense blue creeping shrub *Ceratostigma plumbaginoides*, 1.2m (4ft) tall. Alternative late-flowering blue shrubs include feathery, light blue *Perovskia atriplicifolia* 'Blue Spire' and *Caryopteris x clandonensis* 'Arthur Simmonds', which is half the height and a soft blue among

grey foliage. Many silver-foliaged plants will still be in leaf towards the end of the year and their conspicuous seedheads, like the large, glaucous heads of oriental poppies, will maintain the blue theme.

The Michaelmas daisies (*Aster* spp.) come into their own in late summer and last until autumn. Look for deep violet-blue *Aster amellus* 'Blue King' and violet-blue *A*. 'Forncett Flourish', which is even later flowering. The dwarf asters, like lavender *A. novi-belgii* 'Andrey' or light blue 'Remembrance', are useful for smaller spaces as is the taller 'Davey's True Blue'. The shorter *A*. 'Herfstweelde' is a light blue and flowers very late.

Do not ignore the late-flowering Japanese anemone, which has many white flowers on tall stems; try *Anemone x hybrida* 'Honorine Jobert" or 'Luise Uhink'. You could also consider the pink forms of this plant because the pink is a very cool blue-pink. *Verbena bonariensis*, tall and swaying, has violet flowers that catch every breeze. One can look through this hazy plant to see other blues behind so it can be placed near the front of a border. And *Liriope muscari* – again, not a pure blue but a purple – is an invaluable edge-of-border plant with lush, grassy evergreen foliage, whose flower spires resemble those of the grape hyacinth.

colour boosters

There are fewer blues among perennials than there are flowers of other colours, so blue borders may need to be boosted by including annuals. There are many to choose from. One of my favourites is simple love-in-a-mist (*Nigella*), for its insubstantial romance and attractive seedheads. Others include the pretty flax (*Linum grandiflorum*) that makes fields look like stretches of water. Add tender salvias, such as *Salvia farinacea* 'Strata' and deeper blue

BLUE BORDER IN LATE SUMMER

By high summer there are many blues in the border. The dark-leaved evergreen *Ceanothus* 'Burkwoodii' makes a good backing shrub with, beside it, masses of large creamy foaming panicles of *Hydrangea paniculata* 'Kyushu'. These contrast with the tall *Delphinium* 'Finsteraarhorn' with spires of cobalt-blue flowers each with a black eye. The more compact *Hydrangea macrophylla* 'Blue Wave' is layered with lilac-blue lacecap flowers. In front the luminous blue *Campanula lactiflora* 'Prichard's Variety' sways in contrast with rigid spikes of *Kniphofia* 'Green Jade'. Beyond these the haze of lavender-blue *Nepeta* 'Six Hills Giant' is seen through the slim stems of light-blue *Geranium pratense* 'Mrs Kendall Clark', opposite the massed spires of violet-blue *Salvia superba*. Pale yellow flowers make gentle companions for the blues – lemon daisy-flowered *Anthemis tinctoria* 'E.C. Buxton' and pale yellow flat flowerheads of *Achillea* 'Credo' have been placed at opposing ends of the bed. In the middle, the rich blue globes of *Echinops ritro* 'Veitch's Blue' provoke attention above intensely blue *Ceratostigma plumbaginoides*. In the foreground, a 'throw' of pinky-brown sedge, *Carex comans* 'Kuperflamme', adds just a little excitement.

'Victoria', plus tall spires of larkspur (*Consolida ambigua*) and purple-blue heliotrope. For spring, do not neglect soft blue forget-me-nots, like *Myosotis sylvatica* 'Ultramarine'. Furthermore, do not forget blue foliage. There are some bluish ornamental grasses like *Elymus hispidus, Leymus arenarius, Festuca ovina* and *F. glauca* 'Elijah Blue'. Consider also the waxy blue hostas for semi-shade, as well as thalictrums, macleaya and eryngiums for sunny sites.

colour 'throws'

Just a little conflict is a good thing in a border; as with life, a few 'bumps' make it more exciting. So try to include a 'throw', which is my word for an unexpected addition. This could be just one small group of rich orange, splashed with the brick-red of *Crocosmia* x *crocosmiiflora* 'Emily McKenzie', a tough plant with large flat flowers. As orange is the complementary colour of blue, the effect will zing. Place such a contrast off-centre or in smallish groups arranged in a random triangle at some distance from each other.

In order to avoid blandness, a blue-red – that is, a magenta or wine-red – could fit in nicely among the blues, provided there is not too much of it. *Iris* 'Gypsy Jewels' is a deep ruby-garnet colour with a touch of orange in its beards. *Geranium psilostemon* is a bright magenta with an indigo eye, growing to 90cm (3ft) high. The first would suit a smaller border, planted in small clumps, but geraniums are better as a wandering mass in a large space. Never let either colour dominate the main blues. A fillip of lime-green may also be included, so for the smaller space consider *Iris* 'Green Ice', a bearded iris whose greenish-yellow flowers last well, and for the larger border the flowers of *Alchemilla mollis* would fit in happily.

right: **Creamy flat-headed achilleas, with a backcloth of silvery artemisia and ballota, form a gently coloured planting scheme sweeping alongside a gravel path. Tall spires of dusty-pink *Verbascum* 'Pink Domino' are echoed by the apricot-pink *V.* 'Helen Johnson'. On the other side of the path hang the slim creamy-yellow flowers of evergreen *Phygelius aequalis* 'Yellow Trumpet'.**

vivacious energy

Effervescent colours that raise the spirits can fill the garden in mid- and late summer. Scorching yellows, flashing reds, scintillating oranges and clashing sharp pinks make borders that blaze with intense brilliance and these do especially well in strong light. Such glittering razzle-dazzle is a complete contrast to the tranquillity of the preceding calm mood. These saturated colours are a joyful confirmation of life – exciting, bold and daring. There can still be contrasts of tone and value, but recessive blue has no place, while advancing scarlet is in.

In the garden, it is fascinating to watch how even sparkling colour gradually changes as daylight progresses. During the cool light of morning the bluer tones of red – the crimsons – will assert themselves and individual flowers stand out. The searching light of midday brings out the scarlets, oranges and brilliant yellows, while the evening light creates an effect of colours merging into an overall warm glow. But as the light fades, if there are no white or pale blue colours, only the yellows will pierce through until its eclipse.

left: A carpet of biennial *Papaver nudicaule* glows with energy while the contrasting annual dark blue cornflowers enhance their brilliance.

above: A wide path in the garden at Giverny, France, planned by the colour impressionist Claude Monet, is filled each summer with the brilliant trails of annual nasturtiums. To either side more vivid colour is provided by bright yellow helianthus and crimson cosmos.

opposite: **Evening light penetrates the brown leaves of a copper beech and, beyond, more colour comes from the foliage of blue hostas, sepia-brown ornamental sedge, carex, and the pale straw inflorescence of the oat grass, *Stipa gigantea.***

below: **The large, rusty-red striped leaves of *Canna* 'Durban' intensify the golden-orange brilliance of *Helenium* 'Waldtraut' in late summer.**

foliage colour

When using colours that are jazzy with excitement, it is necessary to bring some underlying order to the scene. There is no better way to do this than to regard foliage as the more long-lasting of colours and use its darkness and tone to create pleasing associations. Green, the usual foil, will effectively balance the strong reds and set off bright orange and yellow hues. The shade of green can make or break the result. In general, the darker greens, like those of the evergreen shrubs described on page 44, will work with boldly coloured borders just as well as with the bluer ones. Other possibilities include forms of the 'blue' hollies, *Ilex* x *meserveae*, like the compact Blue Angel, and many cotoneasters and mahonias.

The spectacular sculptural dark green foliage of *Acanthus spinosus* or *Aruncus dioicus* adds substance as well, and many other herbaceous plants, like thalictrums, leucanthemums, campanulas, dicentras, heucheras, anemones, lupins, limoniums and chrysanthemums, which include mid-greens as well as deeper tones, may be used to provide the plant bulk. Such foliage provides the invaluable green mass that retires behind the flashing flower colours that leap forward.

bronze and brown foliage

Bronze or brownish-purple leaves make a real contribution to the brilliance of hot-coloured borders. Their warm tone is sympathetic, but the foliage is darker than green and so makes a colour contrast. Many yellows are enhanced by brown foliage, as they are in the same tonal range, compared with cool purples. With chrome-yellow flowers it is best to steer clear of red-purple foliage, like that of *Cotinus coggygria* 'Royal Purple' or *Berberis thunbergii* f. *atropurpurea,* and aim for browner tones. The redder purples look better behind red or orange plants, avoiding a tonal contrast.

There are some magnificent trees for the large country garden, that have leaves more allied to umber than plum. Apart from the

massive copper beech *Fagus sylvatica* 'Riversii', there are useful fastigiate forms whose slim profile makes them suitable for smaller gardens, such as *F. sylvatica* 'Dawyck Purple', which is 20m by 5m wide (70ft by 15ft). *Acer platanoides* 'Crimson King' grows as big as the copper beech but again there is a narrower form, *A. platanoides* 'Crimson Sentry'. These two are more reddish in tone so look good echoing crimson or orange flowers below. Some of the prunus are more manageable in size: look for *Prunus pissardii* 'Nigra', 10m (33ft) high and wide, and the smaller *P.* x *blireana* 'Moseri'.

Shrubs noted for their brown-purple foliage include *Corylus maxima* 'Purpurea', ultimately 6m (20ft) high by 5m (15ft) wide. The foliage of the smaller *Viburnum sargentii* 'Onondaga', at 2m (6ft) high, starts off bronze-purple, turning dark green in late summer and adding a final flash of red in autumn. This pretty shrub would fit in with a hot colour scheme because the flattened flower masses are dark pink in bud and light pink when open. *Sambucus nigra* 'Guincho Purple' also has flattened flower panicles of pinkish white, set against dark brown leaves. The smaller *Physocarpus opulifolius* 'Diabolo' is brown and richly bronzed. If there is a wall backing the border, consider *Vitis vinifera* 'Purpurea' for its purple-grey foliage.

Among brilliant flower colours, the shapely daggers of phormiums would be useful markers. They range from large forms like *Phormium tenax* 'Purpureum' down to the smaller *P. tenax* 'Bronze Baby'. The moisture-loving *Rheum palmatum* 'Atrosanguineum' has wide jagged leaves that are deep red beneath. If they were sure of moisture they would also add drama to the already dramatic colours.

purple leaves

For herbaceous bronze-purple foliage look at the dahlias, particularly *Dahlia* 'Bishop of Llandaff' and *D.* 'David Howard', the former with scarlet flowers and the latter brilliant orange. *Lobelia* 'Dark Crusader' and *Lychnis* x *arkwrightii* also have purple-brown leaves with bright red flowers. *Lysimachia ciliata* 'Firecracker' is a moisture-loving bronze-leaved plant whose flowers are brilliant yellow. I would always include bronze fennel in a vivacious scheme for its fine texture and smaller euphorbias for their leaf and flower. *Euphorbia griffithii* 'Dixter' and 'Fireglow' carry flame orange-red flowers, while the smaller *E. dulcis* 'Chameleon' has an overall brown-ruby glow with dots of lime-green in the flower centres. Heucheras are of key importance here. Names like 'Chocolate Ruffles', 'Black Velvet',

'Velvet Night' and 'Stormy Seas' tell you a lot about the cultivars. They all have wonderful wrinkled foliage that is deeply cut and wavy-edged. Being low in stature, heucheras have a natural place at the front of the border and their flower sprays, pale brown or quite pink, are so fine you can see through them.

There are some favoured brownish ornamental sedges like erect *Carex buchananii*, about 60cm (2ft) tall, *C. petrei*, which fans out finely and is half as tall, and *C. comans* 'Bronze Form', 45cm (18in) high. There are increasing numbers of cultivars; all need good drainage. Their wispy texture contrasts with sharper flower and leaf shapes like those of daylilies, lightens the heavier dahlia shapes and act as a good base for those flame-throwers, the alstroemerias.

flower colour

Bearing in mind that all brilliantly coloured flowers need full sunlight to develop their greatest intensity, this mood is most appropriate for the summer herbaceous border. Scarlet-red will always dominate and, if placed with orange or crimson, will become the most dramatic area. It is worth thinking about planting a large border in a series of 'wavelengths' of colour, rather than dotting the selected colours about in a random way. In a small border, the crescendo of related colours could be the main focal point, echoed by smaller groupings elsewhere. So the effect is not merely a matter of red-orange-yellow, red-orange-yellow, but sequential planting using both saturated hues and their adjacent spectrum colours, all with warm tones and nothing too pale. If you consider the basis to be light orange, include perennials like *Geum* 'Princes Juliana', orange-scarlet *Lychnis* x *arkwrightii* 'Vesuvius' and the burnt-orange tall bearded *Iris* 'Cable Car' or *Achillea* 'Terracotta'. Summer reds could be explored, with scarlet flowers like those of *Crocosmia* 'Lucifer' and, later in the year, blood-red *Dahlia* 'Blaisdon Red'. Plant up some *Euphorbia griffithii* 'Fireglow' to add darker leaf values with deep orange flowers, and brick-red *Achillea* 'Walther Funcke' as a link.

Bold and brassy yellows are essential to the plan. Include, for example, saffron *Helenium* 'Sahin's Early Flowerer', chrome *Hemerocallis* 'Berlin Yellow', yolk-yellow *Coreopsis grandiflora* 'Sunburst', golden *Rudbeckia hirta* var. *pulcherrimum,* ochre *Verbascum* 'Cotswold Beauty', and just a small amount of lighter yellow as a leveller, like *Achillea* 'Moonshine' or the tall knapweed *Centaurea macrocephala*. All of these would merge well with amber and orange hues, leaning towards the scarlets.

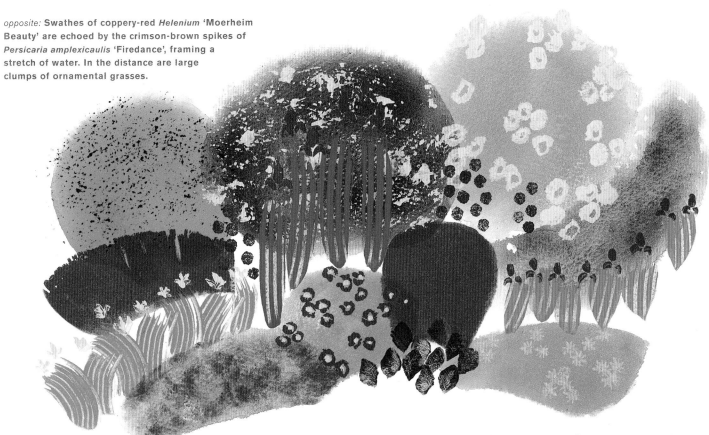

opposite: **Swathes of coppery-red** *Helenium* **'Moerheim Beauty' are echoed by the crimson-brown spikes of** *Persicaria amplexicaulis* **'Firedance', framing a stretch of water. In the distance are large clumps of ornamental grasses.**

plant height and flower form

When setting out a vivacious scheme, take the heights and habits of the plants into consideration. The traditional method is to plant in layered ranks, tallest at the back and smallest at the front. This regimental approach can look uneasy, so I prefer to weave in plants and even hide some smaller ones so that you only encounter them as you make progress along a border. If you have a large country garden and plan a wide herbaceous border, you have the opportunity to include very tall plants, like yellow *Rudbeckia laciniata* 'Goldquelle', the magnificent *Inula magnifica* and orange-red *Kniphofia* 'Prince Igor'. Insert late-summer annuals like giant sunflowers, such as *Helianthus* 'Russian Giant' or chocolate-brown *H.* 'Claret'. If the border is relatively small, you could place some tall flowers slightly off-centre, then work downwards, but without grading too precisely. Towards the end of summer, the natural undisciplined flame of autumn will bring the vivacious schemes to an appropriate close.

Consider also the form of the flower. Oriental poppies have large flowerheads, whereas kniphofias have 'spears' of flower, which punctuate the design when planted at irregular intervals. Monardas look best in a mass, while other plants, like *Solidago* 'Crown of Rays'

FLAMBOYANT EARLY-SUMMER HUES

Filled with flaming reds, yellows and oranges, this border needs the backing of its shrubs, *Sarcococca hookeriana* var. *digyna* and *Sambucus nigra* 'Guincho Purple', whose dark brown-purple leaves are a foil for bright hues. On the right is a tall tree peony, *Paeonia lutea* var. *ludlowii*, with large yellow flowers. Other bright yellows include daisy-flowered *Doronicum orientale* 'Spring Beauty' and daylilies, *Hemerocallis dumortieri*, with paler yellow flowers emerging from light green grassy foliage. Oranges enrich the scheme: the dusky, copper-tinted leaves of *Euphorbia griffithii* 'Dixter' in front of the tree peony and, at the front, yellow-bronze wallflowers. But the reds dominate: two *Paeonia* 'Nippon Beauty', with scarlet flowers with yellow centres, frame a central *Papaver orientale* 'Indian Chief' with mahogany-red flowers. On the left are two clumps of *P. orientale* 'Turkenlouis' with scarlet-fringed flowers with dense black centres. Crimson-brown *Iris* 'Red Lion' enriches the scene, with swathes of crimson dwarf *I.* 'Clay's Caper' at its foot. Included for subtle contrast are the purple-red flowers of *Bergenia cordifolia* 'Purpurea', its large leaves edged with brown-purple, and tall *Allium* 'Globemaster' with deep violet globes.

and the taller *S.* 'Linner Gold', have textures that are best used as a foil. Plants like the sophisticated irises must be allowed their natural space and do not look good when crowded. Think of *Iris spuria* 'Imperial Bronze', a plant that is over 1m (3ft) tall, or the bearded irises of up to 1m (3ft) like *I.* 'Gingerbread Man' or *I.* 'Red Lion'. Their beautiful sword-like leaves must be seen, whereas the foliage of crocosmias tucks away more easily because their leaves are more vertical and less fanned, while the flattened flowerheads of achilleas give the planting a spatial quality.

'throws'

Any border that is so clearly restricted to a colour theme cries out for a little controversy. Hot colour themes can all too easily suffer from overkill and there is much value in the addition of a discordant note to excite matters. Think of the effect a splash of magenta *Lychnis coronaria* would have, because of the blueness within the colour. Dashes of maroon-red *Allium sphaerocephalon* popping up around a mass of hot red and orange flowers will ameliorate matters and link these clashing reds together. And dots of *Potentilla atrosanguinea* 'Flamenco', aptly named for its flashing red-and-orange flowers, contributes a lot. Some dahlias add a little healthy aggression. Their cactus shapes are exciting in themselves, and colours like shocking-pink *Dahlia* 'Geerling's Jubilee' or fuchsia-purple *D.* 'Hillcrest Royal' would be stirring. These, however, are plants that must be treated as bedding. Save the tubers and store them dry, in a frost-free area, through winter. There are many dahlias, chrysanthemums and lilies that can be replacements for flowers, like oriental poppies, that have finished by midsummer.

CARNIVAL COLOURS FOR LATE SUMMER

This hot-coloured border is edged on both sides by flame-red *Crocosmia* 'Lucifer', its tall reedy leaves acting almost as an informal hedge. Dark brown *Physocarpus opulifolius* 'Diabolo' and two groups of bronze fennel provide dark tones that set off the radiant colours. Scarlet *Lychnis* x *arkwrightii* 'Vesuvius' also has dark brown-purple leaves as does the centrepiece, *Dahlia* 'Blaisdon Red', a vivid scarlet anemone-flowered hybrid. At the front *Euphorbia dulcis* 'Chameleon', with massed tiny brown flowers, also has brown-purple foliage. Such dark contrasts launch the dazzling scarlets, crimsons, golds, chromes and oranges of coppery-red *Helenium* 'Moerheim Beauty', rusty-orange *Helenium* 'Julisamt' and scarlet *Monarda* 'Squaw'. In the centre is *Hemerocallis* 'Canadian Goose', with dazzling red flowers with yellow centres among light green grassy leaves, and at the edge a fringe of *Heuchera* 'Firebird', adding sprays of tiny crimson flowers above rosettes of green leaves. Among such strong colours the tall, slim foxtail lilies (*Eremurus* 'Cleopatra') shoot their intense orange spires skywards and the large, shaggy, daisy-flowered *Inula royleana* adds more golden-orange flowers with dark ochre centres. *Hemerocallis fulva* 'Flore Pleno' weaves through, adding a linking cinnamon-orange colour and a curved line of golden *Geum* 'Lady Stratheden' adds dots of bright gold. On the right the smaller *Hemerocallis* 'Corky' provides a strong apricot-yellow.

below left: **A variety of the biennial slipper flower (*Calceolaria hybrida*) offers flowers of an intense orange colour.**

below right: **The near-black succulent *Aeonium arboreum* 'Arnold Schwarzkopff' is the structure plant for this beautifully planted stone trough. Another succulent, *Echeveria elegans*, makes a perfect companion, having glaucous leaves and pink, orange-tipped flowers. Ivy-leaved crimson pelargoniums suit the colour scheme and thrive in the same conditions of sunlight.**

rich tones

Where the bright colours have a carnival charm, there can be a completely different approach to reds that is less gaudy and more luxurious and produces a colour rich with oil-paint intensity. The flower colours have dark depths mixed with saturated colour, rather than the flagrant scarlets and bright yellows of the previous associations. And darker values merge the colours rather than contrast them. Nothing should 'jump forward' – which means including no dazzling colours and few very light ones. So white, pastels, pure yellow and bright orange are not appropriate.

Some colours may be similar to those used in a vivacious scheme, like copper, bronze, mustard-gold, mahogany and brown, and the same plants, particularly late-summer heleniums, fit both schemes. But they will appear quite different and take on a more sumptuous appearance in association with deeper tones. The bluer-toned colours, like royal blue, midnight-blue, indigo, violet, claret and Venetian red, are all full-bodied colours that add gravitas. Choosing such warm, rich tones is a confident decision. Where the previous scheme invigorates, with challenging combinations, these colours create a sense of security.

left: The summer-long sumptuous deep wine-purple foliage of *Euphorbia dulcis* 'Chameleon' makes this a desirable small plant. The cool blue cast of its foliage takes on redder tones in autumn.

above: In a walled kitchen garden herbs and crops have been selected for their rich colours. The pink-tinged spears at the front are a lettuce, *Lactuca* 'Bijou', that has been allowed to bolt. Deep colour comes from dark red-purple basil, blue-red orach and a mass of maroon Swiss chard. The sharp-tipped *Phormium tenax* Purpureum Group adds tension and, on the walls, carmine *Clematis* 'Ville de Lyon' and wine-red *C. viticella* 'Royal Velours' blend the scheme together.

background foliage

This is where the purple-red foliaged shrubs fit in, like *Cotinus coggygria* 'Royal Purple', whose wine-coloured leaves darken later in the year, and the smooth, greyer-leaved *C.* 'Grace' that turns plum-purple in autumn. If you have a large space, there is no better deep purple foliage than that of *Cercis canadensis* 'Forest Pansy', which grows to 3m (10ft) and just as wide. The large leaves are deep purple with a blackish overtone.

Berberis thunbergii 'Atropurpurea' makes a large, thorny deciduous shrub that is rather ungainly but can be clipped as a hedge. The small, densely packed leaves are deep wine-purple, turning red in autumn. Other shrubs can be used as formal or informal hedging – that is, some respond well to tight clipping and others are better pruned. *Escallonia* 'Red Hedger' lends itself to quite

formal clipping; the small red flowers appear anyway, from mid- to late summer, among deep green, dense, glossy foliage. Fuchsias too can be grown for hedging but are more informal.

flowering shrubs

Many shrubs are grown for their flowers, including several dark blue ceanothus, which flower in early summer and suit the richness of the planting design. Evergreen *Ceanothus* 'Concha', with deep blue flowers appearing from red buds, grows to 3m (10ft); *C.* 'Dark Star' is smaller at 1.2–1.8m (4–6ft) and *C. impressus* 'Puget Blue', at the same height, has violet-blue flowers. Flowering slightly earlier, the distinguished tree peonies have finely cut foliage, maintaining a presence in the border with rich green leaves long after the early flowers have gone. To fit with the rich mood, try the semi-double deep crimson *Paeonia suffruticosa* 'Kokuryu-nishiki' or the multi-stemmed hybrid *P.* 'Black Pirate', with single mahogany-red flowers.

Hibiscus may be slightly tender for your site but they are worth considering if the garden is protected, because they flower in late summer when there are fewer flowering shrubs to choose from. *Hibiscus syriacus* 'Blue Bird' has large violet-blue flowers in late summer and 'Russian Violet' leans more towards mauve-pink. Both are manageable for the smaller garden. The most welcome of the late flowerers must include hydrangeas, many of which have flower colours suited to this theme. Among them are *Hydrangea macrophylla* 'Lilacena', a 1.5m (5ft) high 'lacecap' flowering shrub of Victorian mauve, and the lacecap *H. macrophylla* 'Geoffrey Chadbund' which is remarkable for its deep brick-red flower colour, while *H.* 'Preziosa' is a compact 1.2m (4ft) plant with purple stems and purple-red flowers. Its foliage has an 'antiqued' look, because it is dark green-red and purpled throughout the summer season, turning deep claret in autumn.

Other flowering shrubs are more suited to being part of the herbaceous mass than being used as background. Brooms flower early, so *Cytisus* 'Johnson's Crimson', covered with masses of small carmine flowers, is great for late spring. Do not rely on it for bulky foliage effect, because cytisus must have their branches pruned as soon as they have finished flowering or they become leggy. The evergreen cistus family carry beautiful flowers all summer. *Cistus creticus* is compact at 1m (3ft) high and wide, with rich pink-purple flowers, while *C. x purpureus*, a plant of the same size, has larger crinkled dark pink flowers that have a maroon blotch at the base of each petal and red shoots among the deep green foliage.

Among smaller shrubs, the evergreen hebe family is usually very compact and dense; it includes *Hebe* 'Sapphire', with purple foliage and lavender flowers. Smaller shrubs are useful too, like 30cm (12in) *Fuchsia* 'Gruss aus dem Bodethal', with dark purple-and-crimson flowers, or the similar *F.* 'Tom Thumb', with cerise-and-purple flowers. Both easily slot in among herbaceous perennials.

roses

Shrub roses are highly relevant for their delicious wine-red flowers that last so long, and there are many to choose from that fit in with rich colours. Among them, consider *Rosa* 'Cardinal de Richelieu', a dusky dark purple gallica rose with a rich fragrance that flowers in summer to a height of 1.5m (5ft). For the back of a border think about *R.* 'William Lobb', a dark crimson moss rose that gradually fades to an unusual violet-grey colour. It is one of the best moss roses, growing to 1.8m (6ft), and is strongly perfumed.

The new English roses are of good behaviour and habit, being long flowering and disease resistant. Many are suitable for the smaller garden. *Rosa* William Shakespeare is a modern classic at 1.2m (4ft) with deep crimson-purple flowers; the effect of its densely quartered blooms is to intensify the colour. Look out also for some exciting modern floribundas with brownish-red blooms that foster the mood of antique richness in a border and merge well with herbaceous flowers. *R.* Edith Holden is a warm brown, *R.* 'Iris Webb' tends towards a more gold-brown and there is a mauve, wine-red mixture that occurs in *R.* 'Ripples'. Another modern rose of the 'hybrid tea' type is *R.* 'Julia's Rose', with a parchment colour that reminds one of the era of quill pens, but it is actually very twentieth

opposite: **The young foliage of** ***Cotinus coggygria*** **is touched with copper that gradually becomes a cool green; by autumn it is really aflame.**

right: **Rising from a foliage mass of brown-leaved cimicifuga, rich colours merge to create an enticing unity, seen in a planting scheme devised by Piet Oudolf. Deep red astrantias and dark pink centranthus are punctuated by the slim spikes of purple salvias.**

far right: **The dark red leaves of** ***Acer palmatum*** **'Atropurpureum' intensify the purple-crimson colour of** ***Aquilegia atrata***.

century. Being more formal, it is less easy to fit in than the shrub roses, so try grouping at least three with lush ground cover, say a thick layer of purple heuchera or a mass of brown sedge, to clothe the base, with a feathery foil of bronze fennel behind to settle them.

herbaceous perennials

When it comes to herbaceous perennials for this mood, think about plant habit. Because the aim is to have an overall rich, deep colour in which there is hardly any brilliance to jump forward, the shape and texture of the plants becomes important. Consider whether they are clump-forming or look better in an amorphous mass; whether they branch and are multi-headed or whether the growth is vertical, with a single flower among spears of leaves.

Lance-leaved phormiums make striking focal plants and the purple form, *Phormium tenax* 'Purpureum', which can grow to 4m (12ft) in its native New Zealand, is more likely to be 1.5m (5ft) in most temperate garden situations. Avoid a central position that would look rather old fashioned; if given too much priority they would be reminiscent of formal public planting. Because of their shape, phormiums make their presence felt wherever they are, so in the interest of balance, choose other plants with good form that can compete with them. The tall hybrid delphiniums would be suitable. You could, for example, plant a group of inky *Delphinium* 'Blue Nile', gentian-blue *D.* 'Molly Buchanan', with black eyes, or purple-and-blue *D.* 'Cassius', all of which grow to about 2m (6ft) and will need

staking, using sturdy canes. You may prefer the belladonna hybrids that branch and are smaller, at 1–1.2m (3–4ft) high. They include gentian-blue *D.* 'Piccolo', velvety-indigo *D.* 'Atlantis' and midnight-blue *D.* 'Kleine Nachtmusik'. These can be supported by forked twigs, set in among the plants.

To soften these strongly built plants, you might use a mass of several thalictrums as a foil: *Thalictrum delavayi* 'Hewitt's Double', with tiny mauve pompon flowers, or *T. aquilegiifolium* 'Thundercloud' with clusters of fluffy deep purple flowers. Or consider tucking in some slimline *Digitalis ferruginea,* 1.2m (4ft) high, with rust-coloured flowers and, around them, you might plant a group of deep wine-coloured *Astrantia major* 'Claret' or 'Ruby Wedding' to ease the tall spires into the *mélange* of plants. Echo these vertical forms elsewhere with smaller masses of deep blue *Salvia nemorosa* 'East Friesland' or the smaller indigo *S.* x *sylvestris* 'Mainacht' at 80cm (32in). You might soften them with the delicate umbellifer, *Anthriscus*

opposite: **A blend of deep blues with claret-reds and indigo-purples work together in a rich scheme backed by the glaucous-green leaves of iris and the mid-green geranium foliage. The inky-coloured irises and violet-blue geraniums are seen through the rounded flowerheads of Allium giganteum.**

below: **Summer-flowering Rosa 'Charles de Mills' comes from the oldest of garden roses, the gallicas. Its densely petalled 'flattened' blooms merge crimson and wine-red colours that age to purple, intensifying the richness of this rose.**

sylvestris 'Ravenswing', an early-flowering brown-leaved cultivar of cow parsley. These textures lighten the firmness of the phormiums and the delphiniums.

Another shape best seen in the mass is the small powder-blue thistle-like flowers on the branching blue stems of *Eryngium planum*. It could encircle a group of *Agapanthus campanulatus* 'Isis', with its recurved glossy green strap-like leaves and pretty dark blue rounded flower umbels at 60cm (2ft) high. *Cirsium rivulare* 'Atropurpureum' has leaves that appear similarly spiny but have a heavier texture than eryngiums; these clumpy plants would be best planted behind so that the tall 1.2m (4ft) high thistle-like crimson-maroon flowers can be seen.

Wine colours can be found among the daylilies. *Hemerocallis* 'Starling', with richly chocolate-red flowers and fresh green leaves, would be superb in this setting, weaving around the other plants.

Elsewhere try *H.* 'Summer Wine' or *H.* 'Princess Blue Eyes'. And to prevent the picture becoming predictable, add in warm mahogany-reds and old golds of other daylilies, like cinnamon-gold *H.* 'Mauna Loa' and ochre-orange *H.* 'Mikado', both 45cm (18in) high. Rust-coloured bearded irises could be grouped together, like *Iris* 'Bronze Cloud', whose flowers are a russet-copper colour with bright lavender on the falls, *I.* 'Tuscan', a warm old-gold colour, or the 'antiqued' copper of the North American hybrid *I.* 'Rusty Magnificence'. Include some inky-black irises as well, like the famous *I.* 'Titan's Glory' or deep violet *I.* 'Black Taffeta'. These irises fit in best with larger schemes, where they must not be crowded out, or small gardens where groups of three would be very effective.

Three particularly tall plants could fit the rich colour scheme. *Angelica gigas* has deep wine-red, tightly compacted round flower umbels, held erect above lush green foliage. Often growing up to

DEEP AND RICH

The dense claret foliage of *Cotinus coggygria* 'Royal Purple' establishes the depths of this scheme with, on the right, three wine-red shrub roses, *Rosa* 'William Shakespeare', with dark green leaves. To the other side, deep purple *Thalictrum aquilegifolium* 'Thundercloud' sways above soft grey foliage, a colour picked up on the far side by spires of dark purple *Aconitum carmichaelii*. In the centre a curving line of *Iris* 'Tuscan', bronze and old gold among glaucous foliage, is followed by the orange-bronze flowerheads of *Achillea* 'Walther Funcke'. Behind is a group of chocolate-red *Hemerocallis* 'Starling' and in front black-purple *Viola* 'Molly Sanderson'. Two small *Hydrangea* 'Preziosa' have faded plum-red flowers among dark foliage that quickly crimsons to purple. Dots of flower enliven the picture in two areas: the blood-red *Potentilla* 'Volcan' and deep orange *Geum chiloense* 'Dolly North'.

right: **A 'tropical' planting uses tender perennials outdoors for summer. The faded ochre *Amaranthus caudatus* 'Viridis' grows beside the giant flowers of scarlet *Dahlia* 'Zorro' with the orange flowers and dark leaves of *Canna indica*, all seen through a 'screen' of *Verbena bonariensis*.**

1.8m (6ft), it may need replacing as it can die away. The reliable *Geranium phaeum* 'Samobor' has dark magenta-red flowers. By midsummer these have finished but they leave behind lush leaves, heavily marked with brown blotches. *Verbena bonariensis* is a slim, branching perennial with small lilac-blue flowers swaying 1.5m (5ft) above sparse foliage in late summer. Plant these at the rear of the border, where they will act as dot plants, or to the fore, where they are so finely stemmed that they are like a veil, through which the whole border may be seen.

After the first summer flush, the later-flowering heleniums and chrysanthemums are very welcome as their rust colours fit into the riches of the design. Deep purple spires of *Aconitum carmichaelii* will still be in flower and, with them, rich tawny-red *Helenium* 'Moerheim Beauty' and velvety-copper *H.* 'Coppelia', flattered by the darker brown-red *H.* 'Julisamt' add another 'antiqued' look.

spots of colour

Within such a rich planting design, 'dots' of colour can spark the mass into life. *Knautia macedonica* is a great 'fitter in' − with its maroon, scabious-like flowers growing from basal leaves − which can be squeezed into most perennial groups. The flowers, lasting from mid- to late summer, are carried on tall slim branching stems. The clump-forming herbaceous potentillas carry small, saucer-shaped red flowers nearly 60cm (2ft) above the strawberry-like leaves. Deep red *Potentilla* 'Volcan' is one of the best; it is also long flowering. Set some around chocolate-coloured, tender *Cosmos atrosanguineus*, 75cm (2ft 6in) high, or use it in association with violet-blue *Campanula glomerata* 'Superba', a rather stiff clumpy plant

of 60cm (2ft), and then allow the royal-blue *Clematis integrifolia* to ramble wherever it chooses.

year-round edging

Edging plants tie in with a planting scheme at ground level. At the beginning of the summer *Erysimum* x *allionii*, a short-lived North American wallflower only 30cm (12in) high, is covered with velvety-copper flowers that could edge the border alongside purple-leaved heucheras. As the season progresses, the low-growing carmine flowers of *Geranium* x *riversleianum* 'Russell Prichard' could take over, lasting until autumn. If you decide on a more informal edging, *Heuchera* 'Red Spangles' would add neat green leaf rosettes and airy panicles of red flowers through the summer. For a permanent edging, a trim low hedge of French lavender (*Lavandula stoechas*) will contribute fragrant purple flowers over grey-green foliage. The rich mood uses sophisticated colours so avoid a casual mix of paving and use slate, dark engineering bricks or black tiles instead.

fresh and natural

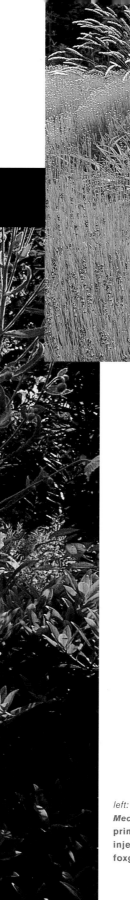

For those who take pleasure in all things natural, the predominantly green garden seems an ideal choice. In fact it is just as artificial as any other colour plan but it does, of course, ally itself to nature. We generally perceive green as a fresh colour and, while this is true in spring, by late summer many herbaceous greens are decidedly dusty-looking as they reach the end of their season. During the summer, therefore, it is important to maintain the freshness with constant injections of cream, pale yellow, lime-green, white and pale blue.

The green garden may be backed with evergreens as the year-long mainstay. Many candidates are described on page 44. Their tonal ranges, as well as their values, are as varied as with any other colour: dark bottle-green, pale jade-green, bright emerald, fresh apple-green, warm spring-green and lime-green. Gardens will appear to have greater depth if you use dark values or will look shallower if pale ones are chosen. Lime-greens, being mixed with yellow, also advance and so reduce the apparent depth.

left: **Cream-and-pale yellow flowers of** *Meconopsis paniculata* **with candelabra primulas are a welcome late-spring injection in association with purple foxgloves and rhododendrons.**

above: **A green 'flow' of** *Santolina pinnata* **subsp.** *neapolitana* **'Sulphurea', with its cream button flowers, is separated from a meandering sweep of purple-flowering** *Lavandula angustifolia* **'Hidcote' by the shiny grass-like foliage of dwarf daylilies. Behind can be seen green-flowered** *Heuchera* **'Green Ivory' and the cream panicles of** *Pennisetum orientale.*

The spirit and atmosphere of a garden, as we have seen, is largely affected by the warm or cool nature of the colours. For a moody atmosphere, dark depths create the perfect background and light greens are appropriate for joyful intimacy. The warmer tones of green – those with some yellow in the base colour – are cheerfully friendly and ideal for family gardens. They add a sharp note, with an energizing effect, as well as implying rural connotations. But for a more sophisticated atmosphere, the cooler greens, the almost turquoise or verdigris hues, are better suited to a quiet mood.

A combination of dark and light tones works well, fresh bright greens being set off in front of darker areas. On the other hand, shady gardens have enormous charm, with the freshness of spring green at ground level before the leaf canopy is established above. Shade-loving plants to be considered for the fresh and natural mood include hellebores, corydalis, paris, polygonatum, epimedium and vancouveria, not to mention bright green ferns and woodrush. All these are discussed further on page 160.

glossy evergreens

For a fresh, light mood, consider an unusual apple-green shrub, *Griselinia littoralis*. Often seen beside the sea, this plant will withstand temperatures down to -12°C (10°F). This cheerful colour is especially valuable in town gardens and is lighter than those other bright shiny evergreens, the laurels (*Prunus laurocerasus*). Both are potentially large shrubs which can be pruned without difficulty and the latter has some forms that are particularly attractive for the town or country garden. The largest is the wide-spreading *P. laurocerasus* 'Zabeliana', with dark green narrow leaves at only 1m (3ft) high. A smaller form, *P. laurocerasus* 'Otto Luyken', has an erect, fan-like form while the more compact 'Low 'n' Green' is invaluable for cramped spaces. All these laurels have white 'candle' flowers in spring that show up charmingly against the bottle-green foliage.

Spotted, variegated and mottled evergreen shrubs will add a different dimension to the look of the garden. The reliable and tough aucubas include an attractive spotted form, *Aucuba japonica* 'Crotonifolia', that is as glossy and large-leaved as laurel. This plant will brighten even the gloomiest shade; look too for the form 'Gold Dust'. *A. japonica* 'Salicifolia' has a natural elegance due to its slim lanceolate leaves. My favourite, the dark-leaved *A. japonica* 'Rozannie', is more compact and a reliable producer of large scarlet-red berries, which makes it a good choice for difficult, shaded parts of an urban garden.

There are several other hard-working, undemanding evergreens, co-operative and constant, that we ought to appreciate more. So take another look at the maligned privet (*Ligustrum*). Not only does privet respond well to being clipped into a precise outline, but several also have pretty flowers, like the white panicles of *Ligustrum sinense* and the classy *L. quihoui*, both of Chinese origin and both summer flowering.

below left: **One of the prettiest trees, the horizontally layered** *Cornus alternifolia* **'Argentea', being variegated, adds a light touch to a large garden. In front is a thrusting mass of light pink-mauve** *Lythrum salicaria*.

below right: **The contrast with the near-black grassy backcloth of** *Ophiopogon planiscapus* **'Nigrescens' emphasizes the purity of white snowdrops in spring.**

small deciduous trees

The deciduous trees and shrubs that feel right in this colour context can be used to form the framework of a mixed planting. A rarely seen small tree, *Koelreuteria paniculata* is wide spreading and has large, light green pinnate leaves up to 45cm (18in) long, with many deeply toothed leaflets. This pretty tree flowers later than most, having upright airy panicles of yellow flowers in late summer. A truly small tree, *Caragana arborescens* 'Pendula', the pea tree, is a rounded mop-head, grafted on to a stem usually 1.5–2.5m (5–8ft) high. It is suitable for very small spaces and has pale yellow flowers in spring. For the green garden, the hazy character of its fine, light green foliage has considerable appeal.

Because they are slow growers, many Japanese acers also stay relatively small but they have great elegance. Although acers are often bought for their purple-red foliage, I mostly prefer the green forms. These maples have such light foliage that their leaves are constantly moving, stirred by the softest wind. *Acer japonicum* 'Aconitifolium' has delicate green, finely dissected foliage and *A. palmatum* 'Dissectum' displays the same light green softness, trailing and mobile, wonderful for the fresh green garden. *Acer*

above: So much welcome colour is provided in spring by ornamental trees in blossom. Here the low branches of *Crataegus laevigata* 'Paul's Scarlet' sweep over a mass of cow parsley (*Anthriscus sylvestris*) in long grass.

palmatum 'Linearilobum' has more cleanly delineated dissected foliage. Others are quite graphic in their leaf structure, like *A. heptalobum* 'Osakazuki', a great favourite, with seven sharply cut lobes to each leaf that become the colour of clear claret in autumn.

variegated shrubs

White or cream variegation always adds to the freshness of borders, especially as variegated leaves keep their clean look throughout summer. The acers and aucubas, already discussed, all have variegated forms, as do prunus. But there are many others. You may prefer the more delicate form of *Pittosporum tenuifolium*, an evergreen that is slightly tender but does well in a warm spot. Pittosporums can become very tall shrubs, on the scale of small trees, but they may be pruned to restrict their height. The grey-green variegation of *P.* 'Garnettii' derives from the cream markings, sometimes flushed pink, to the leaves, while *P. tenuifolium* 'Irene Paterson' has an overall jade colour due to its light green speckling, and the taller *P. tenuifolium* 'Warnham Gold' has lime-yellow foliage. All have the characteristic wavy-edged leaves, creating a texture that catches the light and brings different values to their colour.

Some deciduous shrubs make ideal associates, like the lovely white-variegated *Philadelphus coronarius* 'Variegatus', regrettably slow growing; the white flowers are richly scented in spring but the leaves continue until autumn. *Weigela florida* 'Albovariegata', carrying light pink flowers in spring, is another variegated contender, and the dogwoods, like *Cornus alba* 'Elegantissima' and its sibling *C. alba* 'Spaethii', with gold and pink variegation, are worth consideration. Smaller grass-like mounds can be planned as groups or as edging, like *Ophiopogon jaburan* 'Vittatus', a white-variegated form of lilyturf that is usefully evergreen, and the taller *Sisyrinchium striatum* 'Variegatum', with sharper sword-like foliage.

white- and green-flowered shrubs

Spring is the time for most flowering shrubs to be at their best, but some flower in summer and a surprising number look good in autumn. Among the late flowerers, *Sorbaria tormentosa* subsp. *angustifolia*, 3m (10ft) high and wide, spills its large conical panicles of fluffy creamy-white tiny flowers with casual carelessness, perfect as a late summer pick-me-up. The sharply toothed mid-green leaves and the reddish shoots add to the plant's general informality. Large white cultivars of *Hydrangea paniculata* will also cheer the garden as autumn approaches: look for 'Kyushu', which has greenish panicles that progress through white to fade pale pink. The prettiest hydrangea is *H. arborescens* 'Annabelle', which produces spectacular foaming globular heads from midsummer into autumn.

Flowering shrubs with green flowers suit the fresh green theme very well. *Itea ilicifolia* has green pendent racemes that trail from the glossy evergreen toothed foliage in mid- to late summer. In an advantageous position, say against a warm wall, it could contrast effectively with the horizontal form of lacecap hydrangeas. In late winter another green-flowered shrub, *Stachyurus praecox*, has vertically trailing pale creamy-green racemes of as many as twenty tiny bell-shaped flowers hanging from widely stretched leafless

below: **In the beautiful dappled light of Beth Chatto's woodland garden, fresh spring greens dominate, due to the mass of new fern foliage (*Matteuccia struthiopteris*). Subtle colour intervenes in the form of light pink bistort (*Persicaria bistorta* 'Superba') and warm-toned bronze-green leaves of *Euphorbia griffithii* 'Fireglow'.**

FRESH SPRING COLOURS OF THE COUNTRYSIDE

Beneath the canopy of the small almond tree (*Prunus triloba*), with its shell-pink blossom, are emerald-green ferns and a mass of light green *Helleborus foetidus* 'Wester Flisk' with bell-shaped flower clusters tinged maroon-red. Next to a run of the spreading, butter-yellow grass *Milium effusum* 'Aureum', *Aquilegia* 'White Admiral' and wild primroses grow together, merging into the ground-covering *Epimedium* x *youngianum* 'Niveum', with sprays of tiny white flowers on

wire-like stems. Behind, *Geranium clarkei* 'Kashmir White' contrasts with the foliage spears and powder-blue flowers of *Iris* 'Jane Phillips', echoed by the tall deep blue columns of *Camassia cusickii* 'Zwanenberg' behind. The spreading variegated comfrey (*Symphytum* x *uplandicum*) has cream-edged greyish leaves with powder-blue flowers. On the left the wide-spreading, almost prostrate broom *Cytisus* x *kewensis* is wreathed in cream flowers, while clumps of Solomon's seal (*Polygonatum* x *hybridum*), its pale cream flowers suspended from arching stems, line the bed's boundary.

branches. Keep the soil below clear of large-leaved ground cover in spring – this shrub should be seen. There is a variegated form, *S. praecox* 'Magpie', but it is difficult to find. I must also include one of my favourite plants, the tender lemon verbena (*Aloysia triphylla*, syn. *Lippia citriodora*), with an overall emerald-green character, whose tiny white flowers barely show in late summer. The aromatic leaves are strongly lemony in full sun, the ultimate in sharp freshness.

herbaceous perennials

Herbaceous flowers are not showy yet are subtly effective when combined with foliage. Among the best-known green-flowered perennials are euphorbias. The large, inert mass of *Euphorbia characias* subsp. *wulfenii* has round yellow-green cymes, sometimes 30cm (12in) long; the form 'John Tomlinson' has even larger flowerheads. Others include *E. palustris*, a sub-shrub that has yellow-

FRESH COLOURS FOR HIGH SUMMER

In many gardens high summer can lack the fresh green of spring so this bed includes a mass of feathery emerald-green fennel, echoed below left by a drift of tall *Thalictrum lucidum*, whose fluffy cream flowers merge with its green foliage.

Between these are two massive clumps of angelica, with huge lime-green umbels of flowers above solid ribbed stems. These majestic shapes are separated by clumps of mauve-blue *Phlox paniculata* 'Blue Boy', while the powder-blue pincushion flowers of *Scabiosa columbaria* 'Butterfly Blue' make patterns in front of the thalictrum. Other colour comes from pale acid-yellow flowers of *Hemerocallis* 'Green Flutter', in front of the fennel, fronted by massed cream daisies covering *Anthemis tinctoria* 'Sauce Hollandaise'. More fresh daisy flowers on the lower boundary are provided by *Leucanthemum* x *superbum* 'Sonnenschein', creamy white flowers with mustard-yellow centres. White recurs in the striped evergreen grass-like *Ophiopogon jaburan* 'Vittatus'. The tall stems of *Allium giganteum* support perfectly round lilac-coloured globe flowers.

green flowers all summer, and, for compact gardens, the smaller *E. polychroma*, which is neat in habit and has acid yellow-green flowers in spring. At ground level *E. myrsinites* radiates grey-green prostrate stems that have terminal lime-green flowerheads in spring.

Early in the year, small columbines like *Aquilegia* 'White Admiral' produce green buds that gradually open into spurred white flowers, which sometimes continue into summer. For summer, consider daylilies like greeny-yellow *Hemerocallis* 'Green Flutter', *H. citrina* and the tall *H.* 'Big Bird', or set a dramatic focus with one or three groups of substantial *Angelica archangelica*, a dominant sculptural plant with green rounded flower umbels high above lush green leaves, reaching 2m (6ft) by midsummer. At a lower level, include astrantias like *Astrantia major* subsp. *involucrata* 'Shaggy', whose long green-tipped bracts are modified by ivory and pale pink tints. Contrast these flowers with the shapely spikes of tall, late-flowering *Kniphofia* 'Percy's Pride', with an acid-green flower column, and the equally tall but later-flowering *K.* 'Forncett Harvest' that is slightly yellower. Lemon-coloured *K.* 'Little Maid' is much smaller, suiting compact spaces.

Irises can be inserted in large or small gardens for similar green effect, like the chartreuse-green *Iris* 'Cleo Murrell' or *I.* 'Green Ice', which is lemon-coloured. Massed *Heuchera villosa* and *H.* 'Green Ivory' both have small green flowers. These perennials can drift among other plants or may be used as edgers because their tiny flowers are carried in panicles, well above the neat, rosette-like foliage. Evergreen *Tellima grandiflora* is similar, although it is a spreader more suited to exploring wide-open spaces.

cream flowers

Among the mass of greens, the pale yellows – lemon-yellow, primrose-yellow and cream – fit in well, being always clean and fresh. I use cream in many colour schemes, in fact. I think of it as 'the little black dress' of the flowering world: it fits everywhere. The emerald-green foliage of *Santolina rosmarinifolia* subsp. *rosmarinifolia* 'Primrose Gem' is a favourite, as finely ferny as green fennel or 'bolted' asparagus fern. But the low shrub can be clipped into dome shapes that are dotted with pale cream flowers in early summer. Other forms, *S. pinnata* subsp. *neapolitana* 'Sulphurea' and *S. chamaecyparissus* var. *corsica* 'Lemon Queen', offer similar colours. Early in the year pale yellow flowers also occur in a concentrated mass on larger shrubs like one of the brooms, *Cytisus kewensis*. Flowering at the same time of year is the herbaceous species peony *Paeonia mlokosewitchii*, which has single cupped lemon flowers against a background of bluish-green leaves.

Other useful perennials in this colour range include *Achillea taygetea* and the smaller *A.* x *lewisii* 'King Edward'. Daisies always look right in an informal garden with a country theme, so the lemon-yellow daisy flowers of *Anthemis tinctoria* 'E.C. Buxton' or the pale cream flowers of slightly taller 'Sauce Hollandaise' make good associates. All these plants will fit into large herbaceous beds as sweeps of colour or in small gardens planted in triangular groups of, say, three or five. The clump-forming *Helichrysum* 'Schwefellicht' syn. *H.* 'Sulphur Light' works well on either scale; it has pale grey woolly stems from which come fluffy primrose-yellow flowers. In a large space you could plant a sweep of *Thalictrum lucidum* behind it; growing to 1.2–1.5m (4–5ft), it has creamy fluffy flowers. For similar colours look among the daylilies, verbascums, scabious and irises.

below top: **One of the more charming tulips, *Tulipa* 'Sweet Harmony' is sturdy even in inclement weather. The sun-yellow petal base gradually whitens at the tip and, set against fresh green ferns, both are welcome in taking spring forward into summer.**

below bottom: **A green-tinged white form of *Helleborus orientalis* beside blue *Scilla bithynica* catches the cool sunlight of spring.**

chic and contemporary

Many small contemporary gardens are designed on minimalist lines, creating an outdoor space that is controlled, pared down and elegantly understated. It may be a space in which even the plants rarely change, so evergreen specimens like magnolias or cordylines become part of the furnishings. Maintenance is intended to be so simple that a broom is more important than a spade. The controlled sophistication of minimalist gardens is best practised in small spaces, which are most likely to be found in urban situations, where interior and exterior are closely interlinked.

The colours, then, are as controlled as everything else. White flowers are often dominant but silver-leaved plants, 'black' plants and neutrally coloured grasses in straw, honey and parchment tones fit in just as well. But since we are in a garden context, green is nearly always present too. Alternatively, a chic garden may concentrate on strong primary colours, if the gardener is bold enough to follow this route. The first thing to decide is how many plants you have room for and how many you want. If the design is spare, the chosen plant should preferably be an all-rounder, with winter interest too.

right: Despite the fact that this topiary garden is almost four centuries old, there is a contemporary look to its simple formal plan, each bed harmoniously filled with a mix of pastel modern hybrid pansies.

formal shrubs

Since no plant flowers all year round, for a permanent look you must consider the more shapely formal shrubs and their variegated forms. You could also choose from the more tender 'exotics', many of which have great form and character, provided you give protection or grow them in a container and bring them inside for winter (these are described in more detail on page 172). Some will cope with winter in a protected urban courtyard, provided the temperatures do not drop as low as in the surrounding countryside.

When choosing a flowering shrub, whether as backdrop or for a focus, bear in mind how much flower it will give you and whether, if large, it needs wall support. Plant shape is crucial to this style of garden. Not for here a flush of casual daisies or an immoderation of white phlox. Instead, elegant shrubs like acid-loving evergreen camellias, with dark or mid-green leaves displaying pure white flowers in late spring, may fit the bill. For small spaces, *Camellia japonica* 'Noblissima' is compact at 1.5m (5ft) high, with single white anemone flowers. The more tree-like *C. sasanqua* 'Narumigata' is glamorous; it flowers in late summer or autumn and is highly fragrant but a little tender.

Classy magnolias are ideal for chic spaces as well, like evergreen creamy-white *Magnolia grandiflora* 'Edith Bogue', a tall, hardy American form, which can be freestanding or grown against a wall. For a small garden, *M. stellata* 'Royal Star' is ideal; its flowers have narrow pointed white petals and it is only 1.5m (5ft) tall. Or if you have room think about other deciduous magnolias such as *M. x soulangeana* 'Lennei Alba' a large shrub of 6m (20ft), or *M. x loebneri* 'Spring Snow', a 9m (28ft) high tree. *Choisya ternata* is a shapely, well-organized plant with glossy emerald, evergreen trefoil foliage and white flower clusters. The hybrid form *C.* 'Aztec Pearl' is smaller at 1.5m (5ft) and has narrower leaflets but slightly larger flowers, flushed pink in bud. Both are scented like orange blossom and both flower in late spring and again in summer.

minimalist green

The wholly green garden is the converse of the previous fresh green garden style. It depends on simple colour and is highly controlled, so that design leads nature. Shape becomes much more visible, therefore dramatic spears, swords, large leaves and clipped green sculptured form will have major roles. Bamboos always look contemporary. You could put in a wall of, say, black-stemmed *Phyllostachys nigra* or use a single fine specimen as a focal point. Clipped geometric shapes may be carved from box, lonicera, yew, phillyrea, holly and Mediterranean cypress, or immaculate emerald-green dwarf hedging could be used to reinforce the lines of a design. Any one or a combination of these disciplined shapes would make a permanent green focus and such formality would provide the ultimate statement for the minimal garden, large or small.

white variegation and silver leaves

Some variegated plants, like *Fatsia japonica* 'Variegata', have great evergreen presence in a small formal garden. Fatsia will grow in semi-shade, as will *Euonymus fortunei* 'Silver Queen', a creamy-white and green foliage plant that can ultimately, if slowly, cover a whole wall. There are many shrubs with 'silver' foliage (many are covered

in the final chapter, page 166) but some are particularly useful for the sophisticated garden. Eucalyptus, the large gum trees of Australia, can be cut hard back every year to make a fine evergreen shrub for a smallish garden. *Eucalyptus gunnii* is the fastest growing and hardiest; the snow gum (*E. niphophila*) has larger but narrower grey-green leaves. A small form, *E. moorei* makes an elegant small tree; it grows to 2.5m (8ft) and has white flowers with long stamens. It makes a wonderful specimen for a small minimalist garden but may be difficult to find and, like the others, must have winter protection. Also appropriate here are the silver-trunked birches such as the white Himalayan birch, *Betula utilis* 'Jaquemontii', with the stillness of its silvery white trunks.

all-white gardens

The all-white garden is fascinating because white is in fact nearly always a very pale and toned-down version of a colour, bringing the same warming or cooling effect as its parent hue. For example, very pale pink or cream tints are warm when compared with very light blue or lilac. White can also appear to advance, particularly in dark areas, as we see with white foxgloves in a shaded garden. And,

opposite: **Seen against pink-painted perspex panels secured to powder-blue posts, the pastel flowers of clematis – pink-purple with white stamens – display well.**

below: **A simple colour association is most effective in mass planting. Here, the deep blue-purple lupins are launched from an ocean of white umbellifera.**

MINIMAL CHIC IN A COURTYARD

The symmetrical design is based on the module size of the slim pavers. The plants, layered in height, are dark or neutral colours, with injections of bright yellow and magenta. At the back, light comes through the canes of the tall black bamboo (*Phyllostachys nigra*), topped by lush green bamboo foliage. In front, a line of tall *Eremurus stenophyllus,* with yolk-yellow spires, is fronted by *Kniphofia* 'Timothy' whose cream-flushed soft carmine flowerheads rise above green-blue sword-like foliage. A row of small alpine magenta geraniums (*Geranium cinereum* subsp. *subcaulescens*) softens the edge of the paving. At right angles, two rows of 'black grass' (*Ophiopogon planiscapus* 'Nigrescens') run in parallel, filling the width of a slab. More kniphofias, *K.* 'Toffee Nosed', complete the planting scheme with cream-tipped brown flower spikes.

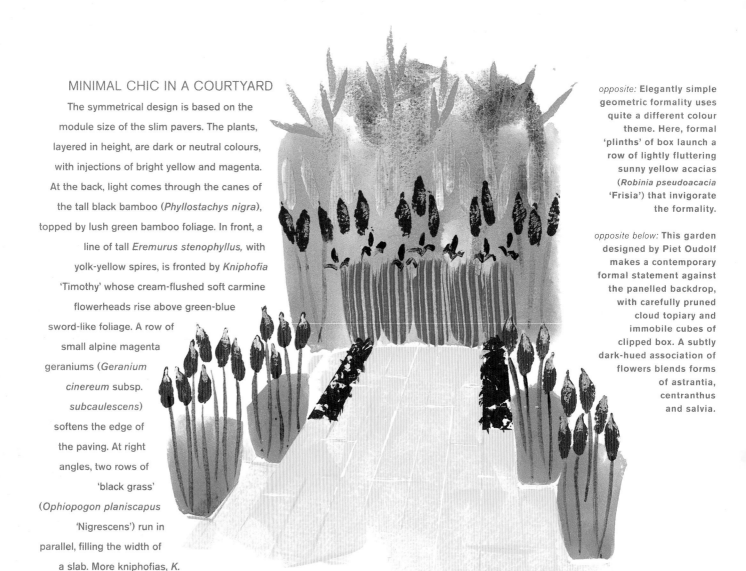

opposite: **Elegantly simple geometric formality uses quite a different colour theme. Here, formal 'plinths' of box launch a row of lightly fluttering sunny yellow acacias (*Robinia pseudoacacia* 'Frisia') that invigorate the formality.**

opposite below: **This garden designed by Piet Oudolf makes a contemporary formal statement against the panelled backdrop, with carefully pruned cloud topiary and immobile cubes of clipped box. A subtly dark-hued association of flowers blends forms of astrantia, centranthus and salvia.**

surprisingly, white can appear dark. For example, from indoors a white-painted window frame appears darker than the sky outside because the sky is the source of light, which is brighter than any man-made white. The white flowers of cherry blossom are barely seen against a grey sky, but look magnificent when the sky is blue. Bear in mind that white flowers also look more effective set against pewter-grey rather than silver foliage.

If using herbaceous perennials in a contemporary context, a fulsome planting style is not suitable. Think instead of statuesque *Acanthus spinosus*, with spires of pale lilac-white flowers in summer, growing from the distinctive foliage that inspired the classical order of Corinthian columns in Ancient Greece. Prickly *Eryngium horridum* has striking green-white flowers and an alternative, *E. variifolium*, is silver-blue. Or a seasonal mass of vertical white spires, like the tall slimline *Veronica* 'Inspiration' or repeated columns of *Lupinus* 'Snow Goose' will add style and may be set against green bamboos.

You could plan square planting beds for plants such as cool white *Iris* 'Mesmerizer', which in California has been known to bloom for eleven months, although you should not expect this anywhere else, or the very fine ruffled *I.* 'Art School Angel'. White *Agapanthus campanulatus* var. *albidus,* with its globes of flower on tall stems, also suits the formal setting, as would *Campanula persicifolia* 'Hampstead White'. For a luxurious feel, *Papaver orientalis* 'Perry's White' has lush generous papery flowers with a contrasting black blotch on the petals. As this plant has finished by summer, it may be replaced by white kaffir lilies (*Schizostylis coccinea* var. *alba*), whose masses of cup-shaped small white flowers among clumps of grassy green leaves last from late summer through to late autumn. For permanent ground-covering infill, try the silvery *Artemisia schmidtiana* 'Nana' or, for a neat, dark green grassy edging, *Armeria maritima* 'Alba', whose white button flowers last from late spring through to midsummer.

left: **In among a forest of glaucous iris leaves,** *Viola tricolor* **'Bowles' Black' appears intensely velvet below the inky-purple flowers of** *Iris* **'Black Taffeta'.**

opposite above: **A secret area for repose is hidden behind simple dark-foliaged planting – a bronze beech hedge and a run of black-stemmed bamboo. The only flower is a white climbing rose.**

opposite below: **In winter the deliciously subtle effect of young shoots presents itself as transparent thickets of simply beautiful colour surrounding a silver birch. The carmine stems of** *Salix alba* **'Chermesina' screen lime-green** *Cornus stolonifera* **'Flaviramea'; beyond is a further layer of the white-bloomed stems of** *Rubus cockburnianus.*

dark hues and foliage

Unless used with a bright colour, or very pale ones, dark leaves and flowers could make a garden look drab. But dramatic colour contrast, like dark with light hues, is at home in the chic courtyard garden, whereas it would be awkward in a more casual garden. Never truly black, the flowers or leaves are really blue-, red- or purple-based but so dark that they are perceived as black. Inky flowers can be found among irises, tulips, daylilies, geraniums, aquilegias and violas. Look at the fanciful names dreamt up by the hybridizers of iris, such as *Iris* 'Demon', a really deep purple, *I.* 'Night Game', a low-key aubergine colour, *I.* 'Hello Darkness', a deep purple-black from America, and *I.* 'Midnight Oil', the darkest of all. The range of iris colours is as remarkable as the range of colours produced by manufacturers of artists' paints, and the daylilies are catching up. There is a vast number of new hybrids with dark flowers, like *Hemerocallis* 'Night Beacon', a rich brownish purple with an electric yellow eye, *H.* 'Chicago Blackout', referred to as 'blackberry flushed red', as well as *H.* 'Black Knight', *H.* 'Black Falcon', *H.* 'Black Magic' and *H.* 'Black Prince'.

Near-black flowers are often found among annuals, tender perennials and 'exotic' plants, and may be used to supplement the permanent planting. Branching black *Aeonium* 'Zwartkop' is always striking but must have a frost-free climate or be grown in a container and transferred inside for winter. This is best grown alone but in geometric planting beds you could mass other perennials. For early in the year, look for *Aquilegia vulgaris* 'Black Barlow' or the bi-coloured *A.* 'William Guinness', where a white corolla makes the maroon flowers appear black. A dianthus plays a similar trick:

Dianthus 'Chianti' is deep claret but the petals are frosted with white, making the petals appear black. For a 'black' bed you might like the dark claret-coloured cornflowers *Centaurea cyanus* 'Black Ball', and even massed sweet williams if you choose the hybrid *Dianthus barbatus* Nigrescens Group 'Sooty'. For height, consider the chocolate-scented *Cosmos atrosanguineus* to add definition, or tall hollyhocks like the chocolate-black *Alcea rosea* 'Nigra' or the new ruffled deep maroon 'Jet Black'. A row of these would make eye-catching verticals in the sophisticated garden. The black grassy *Ophiopogon planiscapus* 'Nigrescens' may be used as an edging to enclose the beds.

For vertical interest, you might allow a tender creeping morning glory, *Convolvulus* 'Knowlian's Black', to clamber up metal beams, with late-flowering dark velvet-red *Clematis viticella* 'Royal Velours'. The intensely dark purple of the former and the regal deep claret of the latter could be echoed at ground level by violas like *Viola* 'Molly Sanderson' and a new form, *V.* 'Blackjack'. Both have larger flowers than *V.* 'Bowles' Black', but the latter lasts for years, perpetuating itself by seed.

If all this is too funereal and you would prefer not to contrast only with white, insert occasional brilliant flashes of strong colour. Choose from the bright spires of orange eremurus, columns of cadmium-yellow kniphofias, rich scarlet lily-flowered *Hemerocallis* 'Stafford', technicolor alstroemerias or gentian-blue agapanthus – though preferably not all of these, since restrained selection is the key here. Inject the scheme with startling temporary colour offered through the year by tulips for spring, followed by purple alliums, cannas, orange tiger lilies and pink nerines.

colour as a design ingredient

introduction

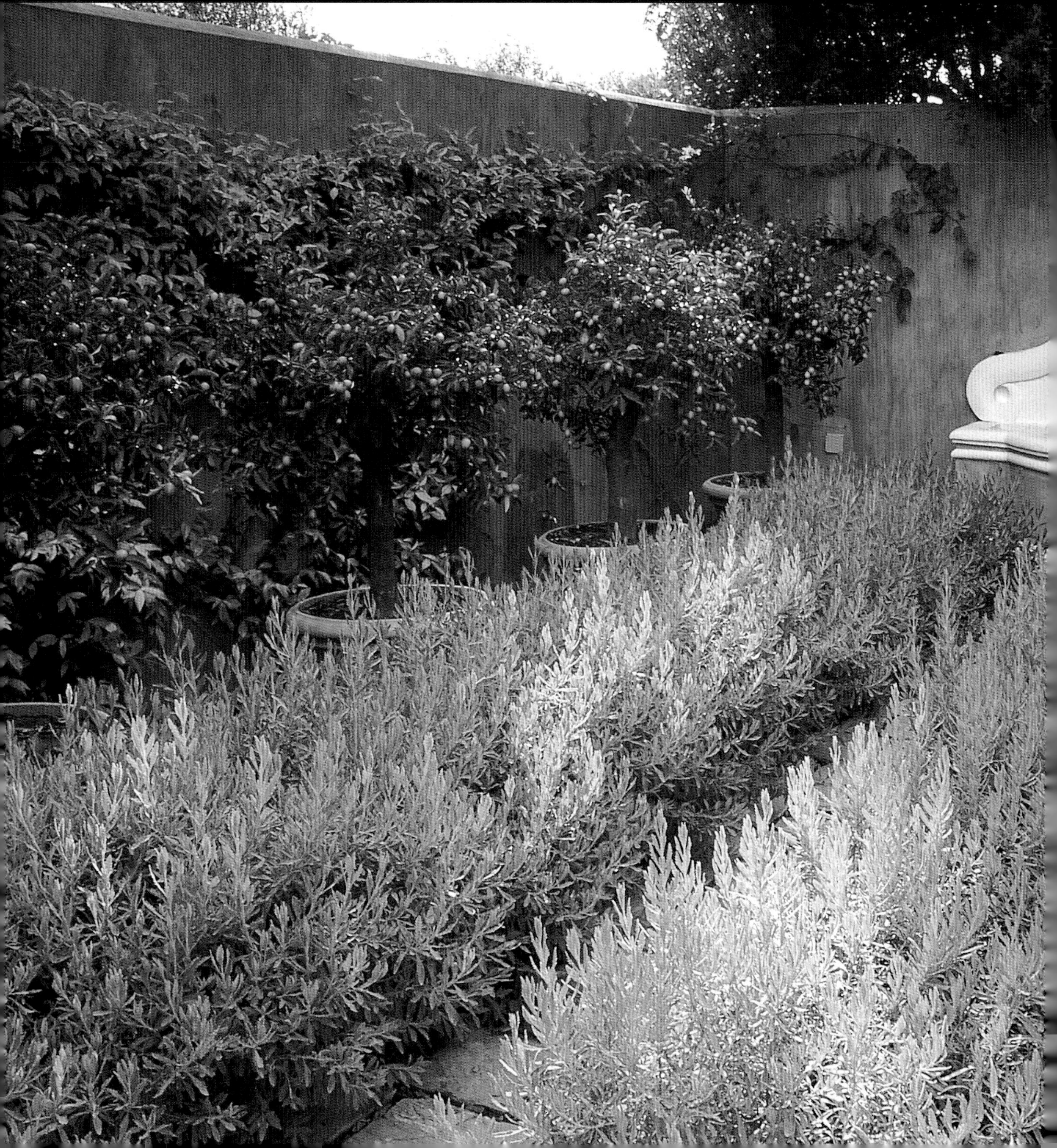

All garden composition is to some extent a matter of creating balance and harmony. How you use the space and the way you divide it up will dictate the lines of the design, after which your aim should be to unite all the elements – plants, materials, shapes, spaces – to give the garden cohesion. Sometimes this can be difficult to achieve because the gardener, full of enthusiasm, wants to enjoy many different facets of this art form. Of all the design tools at your disposal, colour is perhaps the most critical. If used well, it will steer the design, pulling the garden together and giving it an integrity and coherence that is easy on the eye.

To achieve this sense of balance, the colours you choose will need to be manipulated creatively. The selected colours may be quiet and calm or dramatic and flamboyant and, as such, will inevitably express a garden's atmosphere. But they need to be set out in a balanced way, if the effect is not to be piecemeal and even disruptive. So however large or small the garden, try always to link colours across the space. With luck and good judgement, you will be able to indulge many different plant passions as well.

In order to prevent a completely balanced and harmonious planting from being bland, however, you will want to introduce some deliberate contrasts, to give a sense of tension and excitement. The other vital design consideration is to make sure your planting has a focus, which draws the eye and serves as a point of emphasis, reinforced by the plants around it. Both goals can be effectively managed through the use of colour.

Depending on the effects you wish to achieve, there are various different ways of approaching the use of colour in the garden and in the following pages we look in detail at balance, unity, contrast and emphasis – all of which are key aspects of the way colour is distributed through the garden.

left: **Cool sage-green lavender foliage blends subtly with the soft pink colourwash of the rendered wall and the whole is enlivened in summer by brilliant orange kumquats (*Fortunella japonica*), grown in pots.**

previous page: **Tonal bands of colour are made up of sedums, astilbes and marjoram.**

balance

A garden that lacks balance will be restless and unpleasing. But linking colours around the site will help you establish a garden's equilibrium as well as its spirit. Colours always lead the eye around the garden space, so once the lines and spaces are defined, holding the concept together depends on colour being threaded through the garden in a balanced way. Managing this balancing act depends on linking colours and combinations of colours throughout the space.

Since the garden exists in three-dimensional space, we will be seeing many different colour groups as we walk through it. But the eye should be able to make a quick appraisal of a garden's overall unity before it is drawn to the details within it. So look at your garden from a single main viewpoint, such as through the window or from the terrace, and make sure that colours are repeated across the space, albeit by different plants and in varying proportions. Provided you take colour tones and values – whether warm or cool, light or dark – into consideration, you can make your chosen colours work for the spirit and mood of the garden.

right: Balance is established and maintained in a richly coloured scheme, using brilliant red cactus dahlias on either side of a path. Their intensity is stabilized by small-flowered apricot-orange dahlias on one side, opposing flame-orange *Canna* 'Striata' on the other. Dark foliage on both sides unites with that of the central *Canna* 'Assaut', while lilac *Verbena bonariensis* weaves through the whole planting.

repetition

As we have seen, the use of repetition pulls the design together by echoing similar colour combinations at intervals around the garden. Since most of us do not have gardens large enough for one section to be 'separated off' – for example as a herb garden, an area for annuals or even a summer-long herbaceous border – we are considering here the whole garden and its atmosphere.

Demanding colours, like pure reds and vivid yellows, shout loudly for attention, preventing us from seeing the more tranquil blues and greens that speak with a quieter voice. Bold colours are wonderful in themselves but they do need to be counterbalanced. If the sunny side of a garden is planted with strong, bright colours, like pure yellow with orange, scarlet and purple, and the opposite side is muted, with soft rose-pink, cream, lilac and apricot, the result will be lopsided and unbalanced.

It may be helpful to think of composing the garden picture in terms of balancing a seesaw, with children of the same weight sitting on either end, at the same distance from the centre, to create balanced symmetry. But while symmetrical repetition of the same colour is effective for the formal garden, it can be monotonous elsewhere. Many gardeners prefer to emulate the apparent randomness of nature and do not necessarily want to draw the eye to a central line of focus which divides the garden into two.

In the design of the garden, therefore, it can be more fun and much more interesting to create an asymmetric kind of balance. Referring again to the seesaw, consider how the 'weight' can be offset in a different way, by moving the lesser weight further away from the centre to restore the plank to a horizontal plane. Translated into garden terms, this could be worked so that, for example, two bold areas of red on the sunny side of the garden are balanced by a similar, but larger, red area somewhere on the other side. This need

above: **French lavender (*Lavandula stoechas*), with its massed light magenta flowers, alternates with clumps of lavender-blue *Nepeta sibirica* along either side of the path.**

opposite: **Reds and yellows recur throughout this garden space. Damp-loving plants like golden *Ligularia dentata* 'Desdemona' and blood-red *Lobelia* 'Will Scarlet' set the pace. These colours are repeated with vivid red *Dahlia* 'John Prior' and with yellow rudbeckias and lilies in the distance.**

not be achieved by using the same plants. A mass of red *Achillea millefolium* 'Red Beauty' and clumps of *Crocosmia* 'Lucifer' could effectively be balanced by a single large area of red lupins, such as *Lupinus* 'My Castle'. We are not drawn to either group in particular because they create an equilibrium, leaving us free to look elsewhere. Such planning works on the ground because the brain, being logical, always contrives to make order from what it sees.

rhythm and movement

All visual compositions, including three-dimensional garden spaces, have an element of movement. We move around them physically or in our imaginations, drawn in different directions by the links between spaces and forms or by a strongly directional linear layout. Colours can be just as effective as lines because they strike us first and will continue to be seen in the mind's eye, helping us to make connections across the space. The potential for such colour relationships is everywhere. Whether we use strong colours or quieter hues and tones, the eye will make connections between them, even when there is no physical proximity. So our visual senses constantly move us around the garden, exploring its space.

In a mixed planting bed or in the garden as a whole shrubs, being large, provide sculptural blocks of colour. These could be static but, by repeating them or sometimes imitating their colour with a different shrub, the blocks of colour develop a rhythmical relationship. The larger shrubs, forming a colour mass, can greatly influence the look of the garden, so it is important to prevent them from becoming an undue focus of interest. One way to do this is to

above: **The spherical purple flowers of** *Allium aflatunense* **are rhythmically repeated early in the year in a border where the allied lilac colour of** *Allium giganteum* **towers above them.**

below: **Young plants, chosen for their contrasting greens, are planted so that they appear to flow in an organically linear manner, reminiscent of the currents of water in a gently moving river.**

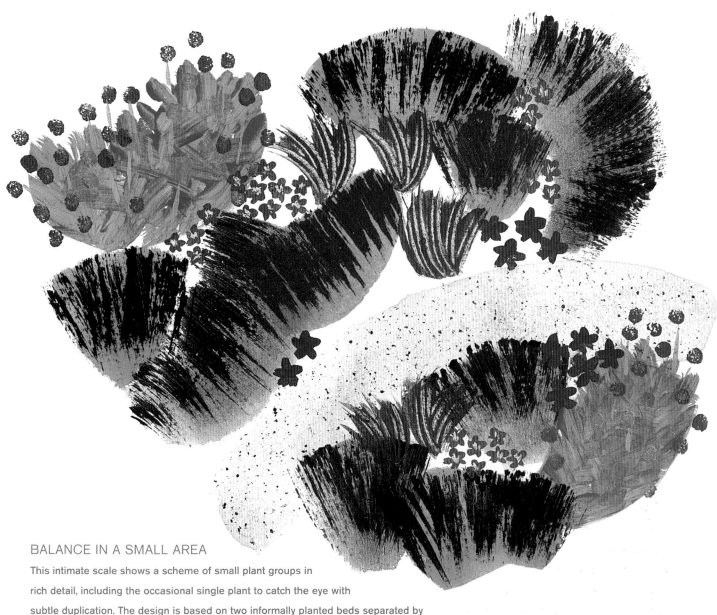

BALANCE IN A SMALL AREA

This intimate scale shows a scheme of small plant groups in
rich detail, including the occasional single plant to catch the eye with
subtle duplication. The design is based on two informally planted beds separated by
a path. Three groups of tall deep indigo *Salvia sylvestris* 'Mainacht' link across the space and the
deep blue of thistle-like *Echinops ritro* 'Veitch's Blue' is seen on either side, with the tiny deep
violet *Geranium pyrenaicum* 'Bill Wallis' at ground level, as if scattered across the path. On one
side only, two mauve-coloured groups of *Salvia pratensis* 'Lapis Lazuli' reflect the other colours
and all are pulled together by the purple foliage of *S. officinalis* 'Purpurascens', a sage with dark
blue flower spikes. Introducing a dynamic colour and textural contrast are the five clumps of
brown sedge (*Carex buchananii*), spaced unevenly, and further intervention includes the dots of
bright orange *Geum coccineum*, an enriching presence grouped in twos and threes.

repeat them in different areas (see page 88). Bright flower colour, like that of *Lavatera* 'Rosea', will always demand attention so if it is not to be the focal plant, balance it elsewhere with other cultivars, like *L.* 'Burgundy Wine' or *L.* 'Bressingham Pink', to reduce its impact. In the same way, flowering shrubs like buddleja, weigela and philadelphus need to be matched across the garden by shrubs that are similar, either through their foliage or when they are in flower.

Evergreen shrubs are invaluable for winter colour as well as for their large mass of different greens, so they too are best used at irregular intervals. The rhododendron and azalea genus, with their very dark foliage and strongly coloured flowers, are the exception here; apart from tall, slim, branching trees like *Rhododendron luteum*, they do not benefit from being seen alone. Most of these brilliantly coloured shrubs, with their preference for acid soil, look their best when planted in a group or several groups, setting up rhythmical associations that balance their strength of colour (see page 162).

Some shrubs are best planted as drifts, which changes the rhythm. These include species roses, for example pink-flowered *Rosa moyesii* 'Geranium', which look good planted in 'runs' of colour to create a natural feel. Informal dogwoods and shrub willows also look better in flowing groups. Smaller colourful shrubs that grow to form mounds, like hebes and French lavender (*Lavandula stoechas*), look more effective when planted to recur along a border so that the intervals between their colour mass are irregular but balanced. Other shrubs with a naturally informal habit, like silvery artemisias, are best placed to weave along the edge of a bed, going deeper into the planting in several places.

using flower colour

Holding the whole image together depends, to a large extent, on the size of the colour masses used. The actual numbers of chosen plants can work effectively or upset the balance of the garden

scheme. Large swelling masses, for example, will always arrest attention, the physical bulk of the colour associations becoming a major part of the design, so it is important to ensure that the strong colours are not all placed together in one area. A large herbaceous mass of bold rudbeckias, for example, cannot be balanced by the same-sized group of soft blue asters because the 'weight' of the two colour masses is unequal and the asters will hardly be noticed. To redress the balance, you could increase the size of the aster group, including some deeper blue forms and adding in a few small imitative clumps of other yellow rudbeckias.

Planning a flowerbed can be a matter of simple pattern making. Examples of this may be seen in the beautiful elaborate bedding patterns set within box hedging that are characteristic of eighteenth-century French gardens. These designs using colourful flowers are based on precise patterns with a strong sense of order, creating a mathematical type of rhythm. Whereas such bedding is static, a more 'organic' type of design involves creating colour associations that look as though they evolved in an irregular way.

Movement around the garden may be either leisurely or fast-paced. Colours themselves can appear to be racy, startling and fast-moving or static or gently passive, implying a slower pace. The rhythms will flow or contract according to the dominance of the colours. For example, gentle muted tints like blues and lilacs should be enjoyed slowly whereas clearer, brighter colours such as warm oranges and hot yellows tend to speed matters up. Whether the

area of colour is wide and expansive or narrow and condensed also affects the 'pace' of the garden. A large, spacious garden can contain all the mixed emotional impact of the slow but leisurely blues and greens and the faster pace of hot, vibrant colours, and this will help to avoid a bland result. This is less relevant in small gardens where the pace can less easily be varied.

To see how this might work in practice, let us take a herbaceous bed with good light. For summer, consider planting meandering masses of creamy white *Artemisia lactiflora*, sky-blue *Delphinium* 'Blue Bees' and pale rose-pink *Papaver orientale* 'Cedric Morris' where you wish to create relaxed areas. Gradually move things on a little with warm pink *Phlox paniculata* 'Eva Cullum', violet *Salvia superba* 'Dear Anja' and *Veronica spicata* 'Romiley Purple'. Then create a dramatic pause, with vermilion *Lychnis* x *arkwrightii* 'Vesuvius' and red-orange *Crocosmia latifolia* 'Castle Ward Late', before merging these with the pacier colours of orange *C.* 'Spitfire' and amber *Solidago* 'Early Bird'. The colours now race along but could be slowed down again by planting a mass of perennials in pastel shades that flower at the same time and merge together. Try, perhaps, gradually fusing *Argyranthemum frutescens* 'Jamaica Primrose' with cream *Thalictrum lucidum*, all merging ultimately with soft blue-mauve *Campanula lactiflora* 'Blue Cross', in order to re-establish quieter rhythms.

As with shrubs, herbaceous perennials may be planted in either blocks or drifts of colour, or as recurring 'accents'. Often their own natural clumping habit leads them to be planted as a colour block, as is the case with phlox, dahlias or leucanthemums. But some perennials look better planted in drifts or weaving within an overall plant mass, like achilleas, crocosmias, hesperis, the smaller daylilies or grassy yellow *Milium effusum* 'Aureum'. Others, like geraniums or *Hypericum calcycinum*, tend to make more informal masses of ground cover. And there are perennials whose small spots of colour have a pattern-making value, like maroon *Knautia macedonica*, many orange geums, red herbaceous potentillas and china-blue flax (*Linum perenne*). Plant these in several places along the border where their irregular dots of colour will help to provide continuity.

above left: **The coolness of this scheme is established with large masses of light mauve** *Phlox paniculata* **'Franz Schubert' among steel-blue mounds of the arching grass** *Leymus arenarius.* **Dots of** *Allium sphaerocephalon* **merge rhythmically into the scheme.**

above right: **Warm peachy tones have a certain appeal: here** *Rosa* **'Sweet Dreams' connects with** *Diascia* **'Salmon Supreme', backed by the more dramatic form of bronze, cream and pink** *Phormium* **'Sundowner'.**

opposite: **The low evening sun illuminates gently coloured carpets of** *Thymus serpyllum.* **Dark touches of colour provide a contrast, with the wide leaves of** *Plantago major* **'Rubrifolia' and the tiny flowers of** *Viola tricolor* **'Bowles' Black'.**

above: **In early summer, the tall, self-seeding bulbous** *Nectaroscordum siculum* **spread in damp shady woodland conditions. Their pendulous soft-coloured bell-shaped flowers are pale green touched with cream and wine-red.**

right: **Massed narrow spears of the rusty foxglove (***Digitalis ferruginea***) provide their gentle colour from mid- to late summer.**

opposite: **In an autumnal combination, ochre-coloured** *Achillea filipendulina* **'Altgold', with slate-green leaves, glows softly beside an end-of-season grey-toned thistle,** *Eryngium* x *oliverianum.*

self-effacing neutrals

Neutral colours such as light and dark browns and warm and cool greys, as well as moderating greens, are always around, in the colour of tree trunks, soil, stone flags and grey skies. They are an essential part of the colour scheme of gardens, adding substance to the transience of the flower colours and at the same time moderating them. When pure white paper is presented to an artist, the first thing the painter often does is to tone it down from glaring white to provide a neutral base. There is a shrub that always reminds me of this – *Viburnum sargentii* 'Onondaga', which has pinkish flowers and brown leaves. When it is in flower, the whole shrub looks as if a watercolour artist has washed over it with tinted water, uniting flower with foliage.

Where strong colours are too demanding, neutrals can help to absorb the shock and balance their colours. So plant greys, silvers, browns and creams in substantial masses where they are needed, to help keep order and establish links through several borders. Often found in foliage, these colours can easily be fitted into any sunny scheme whether it is hot or cool, flamboyant or calm. The grey-silver species of *Helichrysum* or forms of *Stachys byzantina* are examples of plants that will link all together, reducing the threat of overbalancing from among the powerful hues.

Neutral flower colours have a similar function. They can be found in perennials such as light bronze *Achillea* 'Old Brocade', dusty, beige-pink *Verbascum* 'Helen Johnson', many irises like *Iris* 'Carolyn Rose' or *I.* 'Chocolate Vanilla', some astrantias, such as *Astrantia* 'Shaggy', the 'rusty' foxglove (*Digitalis ferruginea*), and some of the brown sedges. Seedheads, like those of the alliums and ornamental grasses, also provide soft straw colours by autumn.

If a large garden is perceived to be unbalanced by areas of unrelated colour, consider distracting attention by planting these 'neutrals' as pacifiers. Try some of the stronger forms – large, dark brown-foliaged shrubs such as the rounded dense shape of *Corylus maxima* 'Purpurea', wide-spreading *Sambucus nigra* 'Black Beauty' or the softer foliage of *Physocarpus opulifolius* 'Diabolo'. Or choose the plum-purple leaves of the tall, very spiny *Berberis thunbergii* 'Atropurpurea' or the large and wide *Cotinus coggygria* 'Notcutt's Variety'. Work them in all around the garden and imitate them lower down with smaller dark-leaved perennials such as heucheras and euphorbias. In a large garden, consider planting a group of the small, pretty tree *Gleditsia triacanthos* 'Ruby Lace', or the sharp swords of *Phormium tenax* Purpureum Group. Such dark tints, like the paler neutrals, help to pull everything together, not quite cancelling out the other colours but performing a balancing act.

unity

Unity involves the whole garden picture, in which all details play a part. Aiming for pleasing colour groupings that are easy on the eye, rather than challenging, a unified or harmonious approach relies on using colours that are near to one another in the spectrum – for example, blues, greens and yellows, or reds, purples and lilacs. By echoing these closely related colours across the space of the garden, the gardener sets up harmonies that are not quite duplication and ensures that all areas of the garden work together. The overall effect is not merely balanced but also restful and still.

Green plays a special role here, being the most unifying colour in the spectrum. It is ever-present in the landscape and in many gardens is the crucial, often refreshing backcloth against which other colours are seen.

above: **Cool tones created by graded colour include blue and white campanulas seen through the erect spears of lilac-pink *Lythrum salicaria* and the branching stems of *Verbena bonariensis*.**

left: **Hybrid lupins offer glorious colours that have a natural affinity and blend well together, including these gay pinks, yellows and reds, with the many bicolours to tie in the hues.**

using gradations of colour

Maintaining a harmonious scheme in the garden, so that nothing jars, depends on an understanding of hue, value and tone (covered in chapter 1, Exploring Colour). As we know, some colours stand out more than others and those that have a powerful effect, like the hot or saturated hues, must be managed in a way that fosters their warmth and vitality. But the power of an individual hue should always be subservient to the overall intention. Hues that are adjacent in the spectrum and have a natural harmony may be thought of in terms of a colour 'family'. For example, yellow, orange and red work well together because red is closely associated with those hues that clamour almost as much. By linking powerful red with its natural playmates, it will cease to stand out as an individually dominant colour and becomes part of an overall mass.

It is for this reason that the moisture-loving hybrid candelabra primulas, forms of *Primula japonica*, always look splendid massed together beside ponds in early spring. The colours range on either side of red, from pink, scarlet and crimson to cerise, soft purple and lilac, and always present a carnival cheerfulness. It is fortunate that some other damp-loving plants, like *Lysimachia punctata*, flower later

in summer because the harsh yellow of its blooms would completely spoil the harmonious effect.

In a sunny border that is part of a large garden, it is fun to use a single genus to create unity through neighbouring colours. Take hybrid lupins as an example. The intensity of the deep purple *Lupinus* 'Storm' would be enriched if it were next to a group of *L.* 'Aston Villa', a mix of purple with claret. Other companions might include pure crimson *L.* 'Red Arrow' with clumps of the deep rose *L.* 'Lady Fayre' to complete the colour 'family'.

grading by tone

Gradual gradations may also be achieved by using different tones of a single colour or two colours. Some warm tones always work well together, like end of summer flame-yellow *Rudbeckia* 'Herbstsonne', with coppery *Helenium* 'Kupfersprudel', lush-flowered *Chrysanthemum* 'Bronze Elegance' and the tender golden-orange cactus dahlia *Dahlia* 'Wooton Impact'. For cooler tones that have a natural affinity, use blue-pinks with blue. For example, the tall, summer-flowering *Lavatera* 'Burgundy Wine' could serve as a backcloth to the bright blue *Agapanthus* Headbourne hybrids. Spires of deep violet-blue

Salvia verticillata 'Purple Rain' and the softening tones and textures of lilac-blue *Caryopteris* x *clandonensis* 'Heavenly Blue' would complete the picture.

Some catalogues may define colours rather loosely and it is important not to be misled into thinking that all pinks, for example, are the same. I have seen diascias described vaguely as pink, whereas some forms are a cool 'ice-cream' pink, like raspberry-rose *Diascia rigescens*, while others, like *D.* 'Salmon Supreme', have distinctly yellow overtones. There are comparable differences among the loosely connected poppies. Shirley poppies (*Papaver rhoeas*) provide blood-red, crimson, rose and apple-blossom tones that are utterly different from the gold-tinged hues of California poppies (*Eschscholzia californica*), with their warm yellow, orange and coppery-coloured satin petals.

Some large herbaceous beds, as we have seen, are deliberately planned so that their flower colours run through the spectrum. One way to maintain unity in such multi-coloured borders is to do what the garden artist Gertrude Jekyll did, by making the colour changes gradual and by using grey and dark foliage to harmonize the kaleidoscope. The colours in her high-summer borders progress from misty blues and pastel shades of cream, apricot and pink to a richer climax of yellow, orange and red, followed by a gradual dimming of intensity to blues, low-value purples and lilac, all moderated by silver-grey foliage. By such means she maintained a sense of unity in the very long borders of woven colour for which she is so famous.

opposite: **The woodland turkscap lily (*Lilium martagon*) has cool-toned pendent purple, pink and white flowers. It will increase its mass yearly if grown in a well-drained open or semi-shaded site.**

below: **Annual climbing sweet peas (*Lathyrus odoratus*) come in mixed but always cool-toned colours that have a natural harmony. The palette includes purple 'Pip Tremain', dark 'Oxford Blue' and pale blue 'Chatsworth'.**

A TOWN COURTYARD

A brilliantly green garden, with only white flowers for contrast, is tranquil and reminiscent of the countryside. Here, a large lilac tree (*Syringa* 'Madame Lemoine') oversees the later-flowering *Hydrangea arborescens* 'Annabelle' and the small-flowered *Clematis* 'Duchess of Edinburgh'. On the opposite side the generous flowers of *Paeonia* 'White Wings' bloom beside the early-flowering wall shrub *Chaenomeles speciosa* 'Nivalis' and *Rosa* 'Climbing Iceberg', in flower all summer, leading to another wall-trained climber, *Solanum jasminoides* 'Album', and *Clematis* 'Marie Boisselot' covering the arch. A run of *Liriope muscari* 'Monroe White' edges this boundary. Partially enclosing the rest of the site is an evergreen hedge, *Escallonia* 'Iveyi', which will have white flowers in late summer. At the front of the garden, at a lower level, spring-flowering *Dicentra spectabilis* 'Alba' is followed by spires of *Acanthus spinosus* and, for late-year pleasure, *Anemone* x *hybrida* 'Honorine Jobert'. Containers add more whites, such as the rectangular boxes beside the steps, filled with trailing *Phlox subulata* May Snow, tall *Agapanthus campanulatus* var. *albidus* and small *Dianthus* 'White Ladies'. Paired pots of *Lilium regale* add fragrance beside the house in summer.

the intrinsic unity of green

Green is not a dominating colour: it can retire if dark and advance if yellowed, but it avoids stridency and dullness equally well. The true worth of green lies in its refreshing quality and in the shades, tones and textures that change it so much.

In a herbaceous border the mass of mid-green foliage found in all perennials, like the familiar leucanthemums, phlomis and phlox, has an important settling role. Some perennials, like the daylilies (*Hemerocallis*) have mid-green leaves that add a thick, grassy texture and I often use runs of these plants for their leaves as much as for the wonderful choice of flower colour. There are large leaves that hold the attention in a sunny area, like those of huge crambes or ornate acanthus, while others, such as the evergreen glossy bergenias, are light reflecting and useful in dappled shade. Many fern-like dicentras are in leaf all summer and, in the same shaded areas, what I think of as the 'neutral' foliage of geraniums will fill any awkward spots to maintain unity throughout the season.

In nature it is green that creates the relaxing harmony that draws us outside – but greens will change throughout the year. Early spring green is fresh and cheering after winter, then, by the

above: **In a damp situation, the greens of ferns, flag iris, tall lysimachia and rounded caltha foliage all merge with silvered shrub willows to provide the backcloth for the delicate, pastel-toned candelabra primulas.**

time summer heats up, many greens have darkened and become dusty. To my mind, the strongest case for green unity has to be that of woodland, where greens of all shades and textures grow in a 'natural' harmony that may be imitated by the gardener in the canopied shade of a low-light garden (see page 158).

textures of green

Foliage textures may be used to fuse and enrich all areas of planting. Try to exploit the visual and physical textures that make green variable and exciting without destroying the harmonious character of the whole. The physical textures are those that may be touched as well as seen, like greyed, satin-smooth *Convolvulus cneorum,* woolly white verbascums and even shiny prickly hollies. Some greens are considerably altered by their texture, like the hairy surfaces of *Stachys byzantina* or many artemisias. Though their surface covering makes them look quite silvery, if you cut them they are chlorophyll green.

above: **Texture becomes invaluable in green gardens, as seen here where arching ornamental grasses like miscanthus contrast with erect calamagrostis, feathery stipas and deschampsia. All are grounded by clumps of flat-headed *Sedum spectabile*.**

opposite: **In early-morning light, the large, smooth palmate grey-green leaves of *Macleaya cordata* contrast superbly against the dark purple foliage of *Cotinus coggygria* 'Royal Purple'. Being matt, the macleaya leaves also set off many other herbaceous plants on the cool side of the spectrum, like lilac phlox, blue campanulas or wine-red astrantias.**

Visual textures alter our perceptions of green leaves too. Some, like aucubas, reflect light, and others, being neutrally coarse, like the leathery-leaved loquat (*Eriobotrya japonica*), do not. Glossy, light-reflecting textures can make mid-green foliage like that of laurel (*Prunus laurocerasus*) appear almost white, whereas in low light the same leaf will be a clear apple-green. Coarse leaves do not reflect light back but absorb it like blotting paper, so use them wherever you would use dark foliage, to set off another colour. These 'neutral' greens do not disturb any colour scheme. Others, like spiny *Eryngium giganteum*, whose rosettes of jade-green spikes around the central flower create a decorative rococco effect, would have a cooling effect among other sun-loving plants. The hazy foliage of fennel, the feathery leaves of thalictrums and the fine foliage of coreopsis have an effect somewhat akin to 'spring grass', which is refreshing in high summer.

value and tone

When foliage is a bright emerald-green, like that of *Santolina rosmarinifolia*, the dots of its yellow flowers are almost the same value, so the two are in sympathy. But if green foliage leans more towards yellow, take care with the companion planting (see Exploring Colour, page 28). Few flowers are flattered by yellowish or acid-green foliage, which tends to make most flower colours look sickly. The yellowish leaved *Geranium* 'Ann Folkard' works, however, through the extreme contrast of the foliage with its deep magenta flowers. Golden-yellow flowers look best with dark bottle-green leaves and the paler creamy yellows with leaves of grass-green. Cool green foliage, like that of lady's mantle (*Alchemilla mollis*), is generally regarded as a good filler – not because it distributes itself so easily, nor because of its lime-green flower sprays, but because of its very fetching leaves. True, it is well shaped and edges many

an awkward boundary, like stone to soil, beautifully, but the leaf colour is neither too dark nor too light and it does not draw the eye away from other plants, but adds a subtle fringe.

Leaves described as glaucous, like those of many euphorbias, are actually wax-coated green leaves. They are not reflective and, though often grouped with silvery leaves under the general heading of 'blue-grey', they are nothing like as dominant. (The more substantial effect of silver foliage tends to attract more attention, as described further on page 166). In general, leaves that verge towards blue, like those of 'blue' hostas, blend easily with all colours. Bluer-toned foliage, like the jade leaves of *Sedum spectabile*, can also flatter stronger colours, as this plant does when its raspberry-pink flowers appear. Among larger plants with blue-grey leaves is the tall *Macleaya microcarpa* 'Coral Plume', a sun-loving plant with huge rounded and lobed leaves from top to toe.

the mono-coloured garden

The simplest way of bringing unity into the garden plan is by
restricting the choice of colours – that is, planning with a very
limited palette, such as a flower garden based upon whites or
blues. Different tones or different values of the same colour are
then used to provide vitality in the scheme while maintaining
continuity. It is essential to avoid any colours that detract or pull
away from the central theme.

white gardens

Made fashionable by Gertrude Jekyll and Vita Sackville-West, who
created the famous white garden at Sissinghurst, growing white
flowers together cannot help but bring unity to a sunny summer
garden. White is nearly always a very pale version of different hues
– cream, pink, powder-blue or pale green – and is hardly ever the
same for any length of time. It is particularly affected by the quality
of the light, so it may be warm, in sunlight, or quite bluish at twilight.
With silver and grey foliage, white gardens are a cool delight and
the addition of some fresh greens would prevent them from
becoming insipid and rather bleached-looking.

Chalk-white is harsh and needs green, rather than silver, to
warm it. The flowers of *Achillea ptarmica* 'The Pearl' can look rather
greyish, which is why I prefer the double 'Boule de Neige' that is
cleaner in value. Softer choices include the milky-white fluffy
Thalictrum aquilegifolium 'White Cloud' and the foaming ivory
Aruncus dioicus.

To maintain interest in a white scheme, both texture and form
are immensely important. Many herbaceous plants, like phlox
(paper-white *Phlox paniculata* 'Fujiyama', for example) and daisy-
flowering *Leucanthemum superbum* 'Phyllis Smith', will mass together
readily. Add substance and distinction to the planting mass with
Papaver orientale 'Perry's White' or the sculpted forms of alabaster
arum lilies (*Zantedeschia aethiopica* 'Crowborough'). Some vertical
forms are essential, so consider the slim spires of *Verbascum chaixii*
and the more solid columns of *Lupinus* 'Snowgoose'. Include, for
mid- to late summer, the tall repeat-flowering vertical forms of
Veronicastrum virginicum 'Diana' and, as a lighter touch, *Libertia
grandiflora* for the pointilliste effect of its small flowers among the
reedy leaves, or the delicate flutter flowers of *Gillenia trifoliata*
'Whirling Butterflies'.

In late summer white-flowered herbaceous plants bring a revitalizing freshness to a tired garden. White forms of Japanese anemones (*Anemone* x *hybrida*) like 'Whirlwind' and 'Honorine Jobert' grow easily in sun or shade. Autumn snowflake (*Leucojum autumnale*) is more delicate, with very slim, grass-like leaves. And *Schizostylis coccinea* 'Alba' is a superb late-summer choice when fringed with the white form of *Liriope muscari* or white-variegated *Ophiopogon jaburan*, making the late garden as fresh as a daisy.

red gardens

In complete contrast, you may prefer the warm effect of red-flowered borders. There is a danger that the all-red garden can look heavy and a touch funereal, but the greens that inevitably weave around such a united plan and the clashing of different tones will all soften and enliven it.

Red flower borders tend to use large, wide-spreading red-foliaged shrubs like berberis, cotinus and acers as structure plants, and it is these that can be rather sombre. Use no more than two or three and mix them with more purple-leaved shrubs such as the large purple filbert (*Corylus maxima* 'Purpurea') and the elder (*Sambucus nigra* 'Guincho Purple') as well as with smaller shrubs like the evergreen *Pittosporum tenuifolium* 'Purpureum' and the pink-flowered *Weigela* 'Foliis Purpureis'. In good light *Vitis vinifera* 'Purpurea' might clothe a wall behind the group.

Plants with sharp outlines would add tension, such as *Cordyline australis* 'Purple Tower' or *Phormium tenax* Purpureum Group. With autumn the choice expands to include large shrubs like claret-leaved *Cornus alba* 'Kesselringii' and the suckering *Euonymus europaeus* 'Red Cascade'. Red-fruiting cotoneaster and pyracantha will last until frost drives the birds to pare them back to their evergreen mass. But in winter the red branches of dogwoods such as *Cornus alba* 'Sibirica' will see you through until early tulips, like *Tulipa* 'Couleur Cardinal' start the flowering season.

Since a mass of red-leaved shrubs can look heavy, allow herbaceous plants to revitalize the picture, with their many shades of red. Among the choices for sunny sites consider peonies, the cerise daisy flowers of *Tanacetum coccineum* 'Brenda' and blood-red *Salvia* x *speciosa*. Add some later-flowering perennials like carmine *Phlox paniculata* 'Kirchenfürst' and *Monarda* 'Cambridge Scarlet'. Through the summer, crimson and scarlet roses, like the luxurious climbing *Rosa* 'Guinée' or the reliable *R*. Parkdirektor Riggers, will ensure continuity, perhaps threaded through with a wine-red form of *Clematis viticella*. A 'throw' of orange tiger lilies or montbretia weaving in and out would also help bring a red border to life.

below: **The success of this large red border derives from the unity of its planting, from the backing of purple-leaved *Cotinus coggygria* 'Royal Purple' downwards. In the centre are deep burgundy *Dahlia* 'Summer Night' with the plum-coloured spears of *Lobelia* 'Tania', all anchored at ground level with dark red orach, claret-red fleshy-leaved *Sedum telephium* subsp. *maximum* 'Atropurpureum' and black-leaved *Ophiopogon planiscapus* 'Nigrescens'. The hot orange flagon-shaped hips of *Rosa moyesii* 'Geranium' and the towering end-of-season bronze feather flowers of *Miscanthus sinensis* 'Silberfeder' warm the scheme.**

blue gardens

Blue is considered a quiet colour (see A Mood of Calm, page 42) and blue flowers are universally liked, while grey-blue foliage can present a harmonious background for a blue scheme. The backdrop for a blue garden might include tall eucalyptus trees and the smaller weeping pear (*Pyrus salicifolia* 'Pendula'), as well as large shrubs like oleaster. Lavenders, artemisias, helichrysum, santolinas and some of the smaller hebes could be fitted in too, but blue flower colour should take the lead.

Use all the shades of blue from midnight-blue to powder-blue, and add in toning hues like lilac-blue and light green-blues to ensure freshness and vitality. Against a wall, Californian lilacs (varieties of *Ceanothus*) would associate well with other climbers like sapphire *Clematis* 'Polish Spirit' or powder-blue *C.* 'Lasustern' in early summer. In a sunny spot the Chilean potato vine (*Solanum crispum* 'Glasnevin') will scramble everywhere, providing yellow-centred blue flowers throughout summer. Blue-flowering plants can be included in the border to appear in turn through summer, such as herbaceous campanulas, irises, geraniums, salvias, delphiniums and agapanthus. By the end of summer small blue-flowered shrubs like perovskia, caryopteris and ceratostigma will bring the flowering season to a close before the frosts. The inclusion of some cream, pale apricot or soft pink flowers could perk up the blue mood – the border would then be bi-coloured but perhaps all the prettier for it.

using pastels

Pastels are basically very pale values of different colours. They remain popular, though fashions come and go, because they will always blend a planting scheme together. Pastel shades will do this even when the 'parent' colours may clash, as for example in lime-yellow with orange, which would become pale citrus with apricot. Look at the radiant fluorescent sparkle of *Dorotheanthus bellidiformis* (syn. *Mesembryanthemum*) and the softer associations of sweet peas (*Lathyrus odoratus*), to see a successful mix of pastels.

Like white, pastels look their best in gardens that are not exposed to brilliant sunlight all day. They are seen at their very best in the bluer light of evening, but for daylight, set them off with rich greens or sympathetic silvers. In a summer border, pale achilleas – from cream to peach to pink – might be combined with light blue campanulas, green-tipped *Astrantia involucrata* and sprays of pink-flowered *Heuchera* 'Strawberry Swirl', perhaps spiced up by jade-green spiny *Eryngium giganteum*.

left: **Irises provide the emphasis in a blue-grey slate garden backed by a wall of cobalt-blue ceramic tiles. Green is the only other colour.**

Varying the height and shape of associated plants stops a pastel border from becoming syrupy. You might include spikes of pale pink sidalcea with the large tissue-paper flowers of light pink poppies like *Papaver orientale* 'Fatima' or dusky-pink *P. orientale* 'Patty's Plum'. As summer progresses, use stronger shapes like pale green *Kniphofia* 'Percy's Pride', buff *K.* 'Toffee Nosed' or the tall ice-pink spires of *Eremurus robustus*. Or insert groups of china-blue *Campanula persicifolia* 'Telham Beauty' and fans of *Sisyrinchium striatum* for its creamy flower spikes.

There is a vast choice of pastel-coloured roses. The pink-cream hybrid musk *Rosa* 'Penelope' is an old favourite; *R.* 'Buff Beauty' and *R.* 'Moonlight' belong to the same group. Some of the floribundas, like *Rosa* 'Apricot Nectar' and the blush-pink *R.* 'English Miss', unify with their warm tones. But the cooler pinks, like *R.* Dapple Dawn and *R.* 'Fritz Nobis', are better kept away from the warmer-toned pastels. All these shrub roses will mingle well with the pale coloured herbaceous plants already suggested, particularly if lilac, pink and pale blue geraniums are woven into the planting scheme.

contrast and tension

There is a lot of fun to be had with colour and it can be used to set up exciting tensions in the garden. If your aim is invigorating challenge, contrast of colour is the way to achieve it. Contrasting or clashing colours can be both stimulating and challenging and sometimes it is worth throwing caution to the wind in the name of experiment. Just putting any old discordant colours together will result in a jumble, of course, but you could play around with contrasting values of neighbouring colours, the dark and the light shades, to build up a sense of tension. Or perhaps you prefer to work with 'complementary' colours, from opposing sides of the spectrum. You might even try deliberately clashing tones together – that is, warm with cool – to achieve startlingly effective results.

left: **Throbbing with colour, mahogany-red daylilies react beside cool pink *Lythrum salicaria*. The cold pale blues and warm yellows behind enact the same opposing performance.**

Combining different values of a colour – its light and its dark forms – can offer a natural contrast in much the same way as the juxtaposition of different hues, and there is often a need to inject contrast in order to give the garden a sense of drama. While dark colours set off lighter ones, opposing shades of dark and light can create silhouettes and shadows that have much theatrical potential.

As we have seen, pale flowers are often set off best when they grow in front of a dark-foliaged plant, like a hedge of yew, holly, *Osmanthus delavayi* or *Prunus lusitanicus*. The dark background will emphasize pale shades, making them almost luminous. Pale tulips in spring, white lilies in summer and anemone hybrids in autumn all benefit from such contrast since none is performing as a soloist but all are linked together as a tapestry. By contrast, the striking form of the dwarf fan palm (*Chamaerops humilis*) is seen all the better framed against a white-rendered wall, whereas the far taller fan palm (*Trachycarpus fortunei*) is best set against the light of the sky.

All the naturally dark colours, like purple, bottle-green, brown, rust, maroon and midnight-blue, associate well and will contrast effectively with pastels like cream, pink, apricot, jade and pale blue. In a sunny spot, consider planting the brown-leaved elder behind pure white peonies, like the double-flowered *Paeonia lactiflora* 'Duchesse de Nemours', or those in pastel shades, such as the soft salmon-pink *P. lactiflora* 'Sonata' or lilac *P. lactiflora* 'Bridal Veil', with perhaps a mass of purple-leaved heucheras in front.

black and white

In a 'black'-and-white planting, it will be the silhouette that is most noticeable. The plant's three-dimensional form will be lost to its two-dimensional silhouette, just like the skeletal tree trunks of winter. This dramatic effect can be suited to small urban gardens of a minimalist style (see page 142).

Black has become very sought after, for it offers dramatic and unusual effects. True 'black' flower or foliage colour does not exist but many flowers have descriptive words in their names, like 'niger', 'nigrescens' and even 'purpurea', all indicating really dark hues. The flowers of the small violet *Viola tricolor* 'Bowles' Black' or the annual morning glory vine *Ipomoea purpurea* 'Kniola's Purple-black' turn out to be very dark purple. And the foliage of *Ophiopogon planiscapus* 'Nigrescens', the 'black' grass, is actually a very deep brown-purple.

above: **The brown-black leaves of the black elder (*Sambucus nigra* 'Guincho Purple') make a perfect foil for its pinky buds and white flat-topped flower umbels.**

opposite: **The china-white, highly scented flowers of the shrub *Osmanthus delavayi* contrast dramatically with its dark glossy evergreen leaves.**

below: **In a black-and-white association, the deep purple leaves of *Lysimachia ciliata* 'Purpurea' set off the pure white flowers of quamash (*Camassia leichtlinii*) to perfection in late spring. In summer the effect will be compromised by the lysimachia's bright yellow flowers.**

Such strong dark colour will take all the attention, so it is best repeated elsewhere if it is not to stand out too much. For example, the bronze-black foliage of *Geranium* 'Purple Haze' and the deep brown leaves of *Actaea racemosa* 'Purpurea' will both need balancing and one way to do this could be with several clumps of *Heuchera* 'Velvet Night' and a mass of spreading clover-like *Oxalis triangularis* subsp. *papilionacea* 'Atropurpurea'. Add in *Euphorbia* 'Black Pearl' for spring, to link in through the black eyes of its green flowers, and, for summer, perhaps runs of *Viola wittrockiana* 'Black Moon', with its masses of tiny flowers. As we have already seen, there is much fun to be had.

The opposite extreme, pure white, also tends to dominate a flower garden, for there will be nothing brighter. White can be the end in itself (see page 106) but placing it to contrast with devilish black is challenging. The tall white flowers of midsummer-flowering *Lilium regale* contrasted with a mass of 'black' hollyhocks (*Alcea rosea* 'Nigra') would stop us in our tracks. The stark contrast can even be observed in a single flower, that of *Papaver orientale* 'Black and White', with its black-splashed papery white petals and the sooty stamens.

contrasting complementaries

Contrast is not just about shades of colour. Hue itself can be used to set up exciting tensions in the garden. Juxtaposing hues can greatly intensify their effect, to the point of making them vibrate and cause a frisson of excitement. The primary colours, red, yellow and blue, contrast sharply with the three 'secondary' mixed colours of green, purple and orange, in that order. We will all have noticed how, by staring at something that is bright red and then closing the eyes, the same shape appears but this time in green. A similar but more subtle effect happens with blue and orange, yellow and purple.

It is useful to the gardener to realize that placing opposing or 'complementary' colours next to one another increases their intensity. They bring out the best in each other, as can be seen when red flowers 'zing' against a green background, such as the flowers of *Dahlia* 'Alva's Doris' among its dark green leaves. Colour contrast like this can be invaluable in the garden, as long as the effect is not overdone. If there is an area where blue is king and all around harmonizes to the point of blandness, splashes of golden *Heliopsis helianthoides* var. *scabra* 'Sommersonne' or *Alstroemeria aurea* 'Dover Orange' would have a dynamic effect. Even when the complementary colours are pale, the effect is still there. Place cream *Anthemis tinctoria* 'Sauce Hollandaise' in front of lilac *Thalictrum delavayi* 'Hewitt's Double' to see the result. Nature got there first: the pollen-coated centre of *Tradescantia* Andersoniana Group 'Purple Dome' is an almost electrified gold in contrast with the deep purple petals. Its purpose is to draw the pollinating insect to the heart of the flower like a magnet.

tonal contrast

Though our eyes may have been opened by 'modern' painting, tonal tensions occur surprisingly often in nature. Look closely at coneflowers (*Echinacea purpurea*), in which the rays of cool cerise-mauve reflexed petals surround centres of a cone-like boss that is glowing orange and ochre-yellow over warm brown. I have always loved these flowers for this reason.

Using contrasts of tone – that is, cool hues with warm ones – is a far more risky business than putting all the hot colours together or having a cool border, but when used successfully it really pays off. You could set up an exciting tension between cold pink-purples and flaming orange, like mauve-pink *Achillea* 'Forncett Candy' beside brick-orange *A.* 'Forncett Fletton' or magenta *Geranium* 'Little Gem' mingled with bright orange *Geum borisii*. An amazing colour clash might be based on magenta *Geranium* 'Ann Folkard', that has

COLOUR CONTRASTS IN A HOT SPOT

In a summer scheme based on opposing colours, the orange spears of *Kniphofia* 'Mount Etna' and massed tawny-orange *Achillea* 'Marmalade' flow into lemon-yellow *Achillea* 'Taygetea', making a brash surround for clumps of cerise-flowered *Phlox paniculata* and rich raspberry-pink *P. paniculata* 'Starfire'. Two aspiring masses of violet-blue *Salvia superba* make their intense contribution and annual red orach (*Atriplex hortensis* var. *rubra*) infiltrates deep red-purple. Central to all this drama is *Sanguisorba obtusa* 'Pink Tanna' with its arching baby-pink furry flowers – as unlikely as a Fauvist painting.

opposite above: **Opposites ferment discord, which can be an exciting challenge in the garden. Here, pure orange** *Achillea* **'Feuerland' reacts strongly with deep purple** *Campanula glomerata* **'Superba'.**

opposite below: **In an exciting combination, the striped glowing red canna leaves, seen behind the glorious golden dahlia flower with its red-tipped petals, contrast dramatically with the cool presence of lilac-blue** *Verbena bonariensis.*

yellow-tinted leaves, with acid-yellow *Euphorbia schillingii*, both being cold colours. Stir in some dark red *Alstroemeria* 'Margaret' with a lush addition of coppery *Helenium* 'Coppelia' and fringe the group with the red-brown hook sedge, *Uncinia unciniata*. Allow tall lilac-pink *Verbena bonariensis* to tie the contrasts together.

A warm-coloured border of scarlet, orange, amber and gold would be made more dramatic if light mauve were 'thrown in' at irregular intervals, perhaps in the form of *Allium giganteum*. In a cool, sophisticated area in which blues, purples and lavenders dominate, with some cold raspberry-pink, challenge the cool tonal range by adding a little mustard-yellow or orange-scarlet such as *Potentilla* 'Flamenco'. This can be just as effective if the colours are pale, since they are still warm or cool, so apricot-coloured *Kniphofia* 'Bees' Sunset' would be striking surrounded by a mass of light blue *Phlox paniculata* 'Eventide'.

To play around with contrasting values of neighbouring colours, try putting two very different forms of the same plant together, the silver-foliaged biennial *Lychnis coronaria* with brown-leaved perennial *L.* x *arkwrightii* 'Vesuvius'. The former has cold magenta flowers, the latter scarlet-orange, creating a dramatic contrast in tone and value.

If you are tempted to try clashes like this, you might experiment first by mixing strongly coloured tulips with appropriately coloured bedding such as wallflowers, forget-me-nots or bellis daisies early in the season. These are temporary effects, over by summer, and you will find that you either dislike or are very pleased with the result.

using accents

Those plants with cleanly formed shapes and clear colours, like regal lilies, tulips, alliums or kniphofias, enrich any garden by providing accents of contrast every so often, when threaded through other plants. Such occasional accents are sparks that ignite interest rather than focal points. For example, in an area of soft, pleasing harmonies, a discordant note, say of orange among blues, purples and crimsons, jerks us briefly out of passive enjoyment. Such unexpected use of colour can raise a smile when planning a design.

Some colour accents are strong and eye-catching – like the silvery artemisias – while others are more subdued but can hold a colour scheme together. Repeating *Salvia* x *superba* 'Mainacht' or dark geraniums at regular intervals can make linked accents, for

above: **The coneflower** *Echinacea purpurea* **'Magnus' is cold pink-purple in tone, but the central boss is warm brown with a light-giving orange overtone that makes this an unusually striking flower. Fluffy magenta astilbes behind add to the contrast.**

opposite: **A single-flowered scarlet** *Dahlia* **'Bishop of Llandaff' stands out from a mauve backcloth of nepeta, in contest with the purple foliage of red orach (***Atriplex hortensis* **var.** *rubra***).**

example. And I have used the massive forms of the tall, mounding, green *Angelica archangelica* to mark a major transition of colour in a wide and deep herbaceous border.

Temporary accents will change the colour of a bed each year. Some annuals, like purple-leaved orach (*Atriplex hortensis* var. *rubra*) or selected cosmos daisies with their hazy light green foliage, grown as annuals, are often inserted at intervals as repeat accents in a colourful bed. Giant silver Scotch thistles (*Onopordum acanthium*) may be planted into wide, long herbaceous beds and other tall plants can be popped into planned gaps. You may choose the tall, white-flowered, sweetly scented *Nicotiana sylvestris* or, for a different colour, erect hollyhocks. There is a deep chocolate-coloured form, *Alcea rosea* 'Nigra', which is one of those flowers that is almost black and therefore makes a natural accent. Both these plants are really short-lived perennials, commonly grown as annuals. And remember the superb sunflowers, now in a wonderful range of colours as well as sizes. The huge annual *Helianthus* hybrids include the tallest ever, 'Russian Giant', that has attained over 3m (10ft), as well as 'Lemon Queen', 'Claret' and intense orange-yellow doubles like 'Titanic'.

above: **Pastel foxgloves (forms of *Digitalis purpurea*) and the soft wine-coloured short spikes of *Persicaria amplexicaulis* do not distract from the dominant silver Scotch thistle, the biennial *Onopordon acanthium*, which becomes the focus.**

opposite: **In a bold exploitation of colour, a dead cherry tree has been given new life by painting it ultramarine blue. Blue cornflowers and frothy white anthriscus set off the 'sculpture' without distracting from it.**

In every visual work of art and photograph, there is a stopping point, a place that draws the eye, without which a picture becomes mere 'wallpaper', a continuous pattern in which no part is distinctive. Likewise in the garden where, though there will be other high points, there can be only one clearly established focus, or 'finishing post' – a place for the design lines to lead and the eye to rest. This will often take the form of an eye-catching sculpture, a feature such as a gazebo or simply a dominant plant; but bear in mind that emphatic colour can be the most powerful of all means of attracting attention.

Strong reds and yellows, as well as silvers, are the most striking of garden colours, as they leap out from a largely green and neutral foliage background. So, if no other feature like an arbour or sculpture is used, a tree, shrub or flower group may be the 'star' that stands out from the chorus. Of all the colours, a shout of red will draw the eye most immediately – there is little point in painting the word 'Danger' on a notice board in powder-blue.

If you intend to provide a strong focal point or area, decide where you want the eye to rest and select the colour accordingly.

trees

Of all the plant forms, trees are the most obvious focal point, partly because they are there all year round and because they are tall and often shapely. But even if the shape is dominant, you will have to use colour to achieve the balance needed. Strikingly coloured large-garden sized trees that are evergreen include the snow gum (*Eucalyptus niphophila*), which has pale glaucous foliage and a trunk that is marbled silver and green, or some of the tall variegated hollies. For smaller gardens, try *Cotoneaster hybridus* grafted onto a low stem as a standard 2m (6ft) high. It has blue-toned leaves and bright red fruits. For summer, focal trees may include the smaller variegated *Cornus alternifolia* 'Argentea' or the taller golden-leaved trees, like brassy-yellow *Gleditsia triacanthos* 'Sunburst' or lime-yellow *Robinia pseudoacacia* 'Frisia'. Seasonal changes can cause the focus to alter, of course, so you will have to bear this in mind when choosing associated plants. For a spring show of colour, consider the magenta Judas tree (*Cercis siliquastrum*) and for early summer the golden-rain tree (*Koelreuteria paniculata*), with panicles of yellow flowers. By autumn, many Japanese acers, like *Acer japonicum* 'Vitifolium', burst into flame.

Having chosen the main focus, you will want to place similarly coloured areas around the garden so that they do not vie for attention with the focus but actually reinforce it. Two linked colour masses, set anywhere in a space, connect visually by an imaginary straight line and the effect on the eye is to look through and bisect this 'virtual' line. So the two masses are less significant than one, which is important if you are planning a formal symmetrical garden. Interestingly, if there are three dominant colour masses, again sited anywhere in the garden space, the eye will always link them into a triangular relationship and consequently bypass their importance to concentrate upon the focal 'prima donna' plant.

You might, for example, use the sculptural form of a silver-leaved tree like the weeping pear (*Pyrus salicifolia* 'Pendula') as the eye-catcher, partly because it is weeping but mostly because it is silver-coloured and light reflecting among a largely green chorus. In this case, few other silver plants should be in the vicinity and any others in the garden, like artemisias, santolina and *Stachys byzantina*, should be massed in two or three groups to serve as a balance.

You could choose to place the focus centrally, as in the formal symmetrical garden, in which case you have no problem where the eye will rest, although you may still need to plant similar colours on either side for equal balance. It is more likely, however, that the focus will be off-centre and it may even be in the far distance or some way up the garden to one side. Unless the garden is really large, the space is generally seen at a glance, so working sympathetically with the chosen focal colour is a good way of uniting the design.

left: **The branching stems of** *Aloe striata* **with terminal orange panicles demand more attention than the red-orange spikes of** *Aloe arborescens* **below.**

left: **All these flowers are potential attention grabbers. The dark-foliaged caster oil plant (***Ricinus communis* **'Gibsonii') with its attractive blood-red rounded capsule flowers and the dark-leaved, orange-flowered** *Dahlia* **'David Howard' are as striking for their colour as the tall** *Kniphofia rooperi* **and cactus-flowered cardinal-red** *Dahlia* **'Altami Corsair'.**

perennials

In the majority of borders the real eye-catchers will be the reds, which need careful handling (see the illustration, opposite), followed by the yellows. To emphasize dominant yellow flowers, bring in the same colour but in different intensities. Use bearded irises, for example, from the intense golden yellow of *Iris* 'Harlow Gold' to the paler *I.* 'Maui Moonlight', lemon-and-white *I.* 'Early Light', pale apricot *I.* 'Peach Frost' and coppered *I.* 'Blue-eyed Brunette'. All these colours would tie together visually, even when there is no physical proximity, and so would pull the garden together. Otherwise, the most striking individuals of the herbaceous perennial world will

inevitably stand out because of their form as well as their colour. Our attention is caught by the massive-leaved *Rheum palmatum* 'Atrosanguineum' when it is in flower early in the year, with its branching stems of fluffy crimson panicles. And all eyes will be on the huge columnar hybrid delphiniums when they flower in midsummer, like the royally purple *Delphinium* 'Nimrod' that reaches over 2m (6ft) in height, or on the silver-leaved *Verbascum olympicum* when its yellow flower spires open. And by late summer clumps of the vast, intensely yellow *Inula magnifica* need space to display its dark green coarse foliage and large daisy flowers.

EMPHATIC REDS

The obvious star of this garden is a mature, strikingly elegant red-leaved maple, *Acer palmatum* var. *heptalobum* 'Rubrifolium'. Everything else is subservient to this small tree growing up to 5m (15ft) because of its colour. Other red-flowered groups around the site are clumped or massed to negate their power so that the eye, ricocheting across the garden space, unconsciously links all three in a triangular relationship. On the left at the front is a group of *Kniphofia* 'Prince Igor', a 1.8m (6ft) red giant of a plant, echoed on the opposite side by a clump of flaming *Crocosmia* 'Lucifer', while closer to the tree is a mass of *Monarda* 'Gardenview Scarlet'. The eye looks at none of these herbaceous clumps as the priority but links them in a triangluar relationship, creating a balance. Their connection thus ensures that none of them will distract from the garden's main focus, the Japanese maple.

colour in context

Gardens are the sum of many parts. The size of the garden will affect the scale of the planting design and this in turn suggests different approaches to using colour. If you compare the impact of a large abstract oil painting, where the brush may be large and the colour massed and thick, with the delicacy of small watercolours whose details are best seen close to, this is indicative of the difference between the use of colour in a large garden and in a more intimate space.

The volume of colour, as well as its quality, suits different scales of garden. In the larger space there is scope for wide, swinging colour masses, like sweeps of Michaelmas daisies, a large clump of lupins or swathes of coneflowers or rudbeckias. In smaller spaces there is no room for such bulk and the considerations are entirely different. Here the proportions of flower colour are reduced in order to relate to the scale of the more compact garden, but detail becomes more relevant, especially near the house. On the whole, the smaller the site, the more interesting the detail should be, so plants with a delicate structure, like aquilegias or eryngiums, are properly appreciated at close quarters.

right: **In a small urban garden that makes full use of boundary walls, the beauty of colour detail is clearly seen in the combination of *Clematis* 'Niobe' with the evergreen wall shrub *Escallonia* 'Pride of Donard'.**

previous page: **Part of a large country garden shows a mass of highly colourful plants native to Crete, creating the effect of a Cretan meadow. All depend upon sunlight and ground that drains freely.**

larger gardens

The larger garden is likely to be in a rural setting where the greens of the surrounding countryside are the unifying force. Inside the boundaries, nature mingles with artifice and this needs subtle handling. If the countryside is part of the view, the colours in the garden should relate to it, whereas when the garden is entirely enclosed and the landscape not visible, then the garden can be a work of art in itself, with no outside references. But when, as happens all too often, a brilliantly hued 'suburban' style of garden is transferred to a rural area, the contrast of strongly coloured cultivars against the gentle greens or browns of the landscape can be jarring.

With a new country garden, the aim should be to make it merge comfortably with the colours of the rural surroundings. The first decision therefore concerns the boundaries. Are they to be open and the views beyond treasured? Or is the space to be enclosed with rural hedging and views and vistas only glimpsed? If the garden flows directly into countryside, let green be the link, with subtly coloured flowers and shrubs that merge easily with the background, like elders, the guelder rose, wild species roses and shrubby willows. Or, bearing in mind that wind is the gardener's enemy, plant hedges of blackthorn, hawthorn, yew, spindle bushes or dog roses, always working with the soil type so that chalk-loving plants are not mixed with those that prefer acid conditions. Trees will have a major role in a large garden, guiding the eye skywards. Here again, it is best to avoid glamorous hybrids that are 'foreign' to the area, for example the golden robinia or Japanese acer in a north European landscape. Both the shape and the colours would clash. Aim instead for native species in most shades and tones of green.

right: **Trees beyond the open boundaries become part of the garden picture. In the distance, cream thalictrum merges into green foliage and does not compete with the generous masses of delphiniums and the hot red of poppies close by.**

colour and distance

Sensitivity to the landscape is always important. The poet William Wordsworth railed against white as a colour for the houses in the English Lake District because it made them too obtrusive. White remains visible in the far distance and in this landscape renowned for its wild beauty he preferred to see the deeper shades of warm-toned earth colours. Distance affects the appearance of colours so much that those which normally stand out may appear to retreat, being paled and blued into the landscape. Think of the 'blue' of islands seen across the sea or of far-away mountains. Cool colours become even paler with distance, and even the brighter colours are dimmed. Blue is a space-enhancing colour, which is why massed blue flowers at the far end of a garden extend its apparent length.

Dark colours also tend to retreat – and they may not necessarily be green. For example red- or purple-leaved shrubs, like a group of dark, wide-spreading *Cercis canadensis* 'Forest Pansy', can imply greater depth by pushing the boundaries further away. If, on the other hand, the massed foliage colour is brighter and more eye-catching, such as a run of variegated dogwoods like *Cornus alba* 'Spaethii', it is a good idea to make the group smaller than that of the darker shrubs so that it does not appear to jump forward. On this premise, always consider the size of the colour mass if you want to make a virtue of deep space.

Bright, saturated colours, by contrast, always tend to advance so even a distant clump of rudbeckias will appear to leap into the foreground for attention; if the clump is very large, it will greatly foreshorten the apparent depth of the space. Seen close to, all colours are more intense, since they are not quietened down by the scattering of blue light that affects distance, and this can be exploited in smaller spaces (see page 138).

opposite: **A shaft of evening light illuminates the far end of a large garden, but massed cerise** *Monarda* **'Cambridge Scarlet' still dominates among the quieter drifts of astrantias, seen with the slim spires of white** *Verbascum chaixii* **'Album' and the pink-buff inflorescences of** *Calamagrostis x acutiflora* **'Karl Foerster'.**

left: **The far trees are blued by distance but, close to, golden** *Rudbeckia laciniata* **'Hortensia', lemon-yellow** *Crocosmia* **'Golden Fleece' and pink echinaceas still hold attention in late summer.**

light

Light is a major consideration in any garden. The decision about where to place trees is in large part to do with light and shade. If the large garden is to be an attractive space, some areas of shade are a good idea. These can be created by planting a group of trees as a dense canopy – perhaps a few Indian horse chestnuts (*Aesculus indica* 'Sydney Pearce'), a 15m (50ft) high tree with good leaf colour in spring and autumn, plus flowers in spring. For a less substantial leaf canopy that will create lighter, dappled shade, you might choose the Swedish birch (*Betula pendula* 'Dalecarlica'); these are so slim that they can be planted quite close together, allowing a greater number to be grouped.

proportion and plant mass

The scale of the garden will automatically suggest proportions of colour and numbers of plants, but one of the first big decisions is how large the area of flat green – the lawn or grass – will be. Then consider how much screening with shrubs and trees is required and which of these will be evergreen. Decide also which shrubs will be planted in multiples. Solid colour masses from deciduous shrubs like green or golden elders (*Sambucus*) are achieved by grouping several close together, with single specimens placed elsewhere to link with the overall mass.

Having made basic layout decisions, the proportions of plant colour can assessed. The size of a block of colour will depend on its importance and the distance from the house. In a large space, sweeping masses of colour make a more effective backdrop than timid blocks. Big, bold herbaceous swathes might be planted in the domestic garden, using a single perennial, for example strong yellow heleniums or solidago. Seen from a distance, these will balance the power of massed shrubs, being long in flower and having similar bulk. Such washes of bold colour, seen across the space of a large garden, will be blurred in their detail but are fundamental in the structural design of the larger garden space. Other substantial areas of colour might be based on bold red cultivars of *Phlox paniculata* or on a paler colour such as cream *Aruncus dioicus*.

The same plant does not necessarily have to be repeated either. The sweeps of colour can be planned so that the eye progresses down a tiered mass planting, possibly including chrome-yellow

AUTUMN COLOURS IN A LARGE GARDEN

Part of a larger garden provides the chance to create an autumnal scene. Blazing colour is established
by trees like *Amelanchier lamarckii* on the left and the cherry, *Prunus* 'Shirofugen', on the right. The purple-
leaved *Cercis canadensis* 'Forest Pansy', top right, has warmed to crimson, as has the red-leaved *Cotinus*
'Grace' at the far end of the pergola. The flowering shrubs *Hydrangea paniculata* 'Pink Diamond' and *Hibiscus
syriacus* 'Blue Bird' are in full flower, and *Potentilla fruticosa* 'Tangerine' and *Choisya* 'Aztec Pearl' still have
some blooms. Perennials like *Monarda* 'Croftway Pink', *Aster* 'Rose Bonnet', red *Schizostylis coccinea* 'Major',
russet-coloured *Helenium* 'Moerheim Beauty', cool yellow *Phygelius aequalis* 'Yellow Trumpet', dark *Caryopteris
x clandonensis* 'Heavenly Blue', mid-blue *Agapanthus* Headbourne hybrids and bright blue *Aster frikartii*
'Mönch' all provide late colour. Below the amelanchier, massed white *Anemone x hybrida* 'Honorine Jobert' is
balanced across the garden by a run of grassy *Liriope muscari* 'Munroe White'. Brown sedge and plum-purple
Sedum spectabile 'Autumn Joy' enrich the scheme. The scarlet fruits on the small tree *Cotoneaster lacteus* and
the nearby shrub roses, *Rosa moyesii* 'Geranium', oppose those of *Pyracantha* 'Mohave' on the other side. Over
the pergola the foliage of *Vitis vinifera* 'Purpurea' has just turned claret-red, balancing the colour on the other
boundary of *Clematis viticella* 'Purpurea Plena Elegans'.

Achillea x *filipendulina* 'Gold Plate', tall golden *Hemerocallis* 'Berlin Yellow', rods of pale yellow *Phlomis russeliana* and tall airy flowers of creamy *Artemisia lactiflora*. The size of garden will influence the chosen proportions of the drifts. Make sure the distant spreads of colour are not too thin or they will not be seen properly. Since a sense of unity matters in the large garden scene (see page 98), try to repeat hues, tones and shades at intervals to create linked rhythms around the garden space. Colour that is thoughtlessly dotted around makes for a restless scene because there is nowhere for the eye to pause. On the other hand, it is important that no single colour group stands out too much unless it is to be the focal area of the garden.

harmonious large beds

Even in a really spacious site, the scheme can still be serene, with several large plant groups and swirling masses of colour. As an example I suggest a blue scheme that will not push for attention, with some pale yellow added as a counterbalance. The focal plant could be several clumps, planted at intervals, of the silvery cardoon (*Cynara cardunculus*) that has strong stems with iridescent violet-blue thistle flowers over arching, boldly incised leaves. Surround this with tall catmint (*Nepeta* 'Six Hills Giant') and match both these elsewhere in the garden with several groups of *Campanula lactiflora* 'Prichard's Variety', a herbaceous perennial with densely packed luminous light blue flowers that grows to about 1m (3ft). Perhaps you could include nearby several clusters of lavender-blue *Phlox paniculata* 'Toits de Paris', behind which you might place the bushy

light yellow tree lupin (*Lupinus arboreus*), growing to 2m (6ft) high and wide.

Work into this large scheme some cream and green flower colour as drifts, like *Nepeta govaniana*, with airy pale yellow flowers in summer, or clumps of *Aruncus dioicus*, whose creamy plumes grow above light green lush foliage. The larger the clump of the focal plant, the more other plants should weave through it. Interweaving plants creates a gentle effect and *Phlomis russeliana*, with its tall stems of pale yellow flower whorls at regular intervals, is ideal. At its foot, and serving as an edging, the green frilled leaves of *Teucrium scorodonia* 'Crispum Marginatum' would complete the tranquil flower border.

Alternative to the cardoon, focal plants with distinctive form and leaves could include the massive green leaves of white-flowered *Crambe cordifolia* and of *Angelica archangelica*, with stylish green umbels in summer. Or you might look at the pewter-grey plume poppy (*Macleaya cordata*) and the tender silvery leaved *Melianthus major*. Many such plants have leaves down to the ground, in which case do not obscure them by placing fussy plants in front.

above right: **Rudbeckia fulgida** *var.* **sullivantii 'Goldsturm' has golden flowers well into late summer. It is clear why it has earned the nickname 'Black-eyed Susan'.**

right: **Sweeps of yellow, made up of lime-yellow** *Solidago* **'Goldenmosa', daisy-flowered gold** *Coreopsis auriculata* **'Schnittgold', the sharp, sulphurous** *Euphorbia wallichii* **and amber** *Ligularia dentata* **'Desdemona', are sympathetic to the hot flame colours of red** *Crocosmia* **'Fireglow'. But it is the dark foliage of the young fastigiate copper beech,** *Fagus sylvatica* **'Dawyck Purple', that anchors this large mass together.**

herbaceous borders

Only in the larger garden is there enough space for parallel or single herbaceous borders. They need a spacious site as they should never be less that 3m (10ft) deep, and preferably deeper. This way there is enough room for the massive individual plants to have other plants in front of them and those that look better mingling with the clumps can weave in and out of the whole *mélange*. Though this is a high-maintenance style of gardening, herbaceous borders are a wonderful chance to really enjoy colour.

If there is room for only one border, I suggest this does not run at right angles to the house as it cannot be satisfactorily balanced on the other side. Consider planning a border with a swinging curve, backed by a yew hedge, with glimpses of tall shrubs and trees behind, implying a larger garden space. In parallel beds, the colours need to link across, not by duplication but by including plants of the same colour at irregular intervals so the eye establishes a unity.

There are different approaches to the herbaceous border. For example, the colour theme can be restricted to a single hue, like a red border (see page 107), or many gardeners favour a bi-coloured theme like blues with yellow, cream and orange. But for me, the best herbaceous grouping is one that celebrates the vast range of colours available among herbaceous perennials and here you will have all the room you need to display them. In this case, planning depends on using the green background as a foil and exploiting the values and tones of colour for emphasis. Echo similar colours, repeating some plants in groups or sweeps that interlink, and change colour gradually as the border lengthens (see page 101). Vary the size of the colour blocks to emphasize a particular colour and let smaller proportions pick up a different theme elsewhere.

Bear in mind the richness of form and texture that enhances a mass of herbaceous plants, from the erect, vertical veronicastrums or verbascums to the fluffy nature of the moisture-loving *Filipendula purpurea* or, for dryer soils, the deep purple *Thalictrum aquilegifolium* 'Thundercloud' or the insubstantial creamy flowers of tall *Stipa gigantea*. Some neutrally coloured masses, like *Artemisia lactiflora*, that do not stand out as individuals, are most effective as a textural mass wending their way through these sun-filled borders. Tall and widely branching, at the end of the summer the artemisia's dark green stems underpin creamy white panicles. The form Guizhou Group has purple stems and foliage that add depth and warmth to the border. Include seasonal spots of colour, like tulips in spring, alliums and lilies for summer, then pink nerines and red schizostylis. Many late-summer and autumn perennials can fill any gaps: choose from anemone hybrids, eupatorium, chrysanthemums and dahlias.

above: **In a detail from a large garden soft bluish light illuminates erect lavender-blue irises, their vertical form imitated by tall wine-red lupins. The blues are seen again in the mass of blue geraniums and cornflowers. Such cool tones are maintained by the cold pink spires of *Persicaria bistorta* 'Superba', that also rhythmically echoes the other vertical forms.**

opposite above: **This magnificent herbaceous border made up of all colours is successfully managed by echoing the colour of blue salvias with clumps of delphiniums and cool pink geraniums that link tonally. There are warming colours too, like rich yellow daylilies, the golden-leaved *Lonicera nitida* 'Baggesen's Gold' and, further along, a small yellow sedge. White gypsophila fits in easily.**

opposite below: **Evening light through the trees creates a theatrical backcloth against which tall spires of yellow *Ligularia* 'The Rocket' and young miscanthus foliage are lit up. They contrast effectively with a mass of *Monarda* 'Cambridge Scarlet'. In the distance the luminous silvery small tree *Elaeagnus angustifolia* emphasizes the sense of spaciousness.**

The gardens we are considering here are in fact the majority of domestic or suburban gardens, those that are neither large country estates nor tiny urban courtyards. In such gardens many of us have enough space to really enjoy plants without having to contend with the restrictions imposed by the compact dimensions of small enclosed city plots.

above: Subtle associations are at work in a small garden where lush green foliage binds many colours together. Self-sown single pink annual poppies are echoed by pink achilleas while the sharp yellow of tall slim lysimachias are reflected by butter-yellow verbascums. An orange climbing rose is also colour related to apricot alstroemerias. White flowers occur at intervals, like the chalky shasta daisies, cream verbascums and fluffy ivory aruncus. Note how the shapes of the perennials, as well as their colours, create repeated rhythms.

right: The full beauty of a planting association is seen close to as the delicate lilac-mauve flowers of *Origanum laevigatum* 'Herrenhausen' spike the raspberry-pink flattened flowerheads of *Sedum* 'Autumn Joy', which are about to open.

The colours here harmonize as cool tones. They are mostly blues with wine-red, pink and purple. At the top is *Hebe franciscana* 'Blue Gem', a compact domed evergreen shrub with bright blue racemes. To its left is the taller *Phlox paniculata* 'Eva Cullum' whose rich pink flowers have a dark eye, and, taller again, *Iris sibirica* 'Orville Fay' with deep purple flowers. In front, the small grey-leaved *Lavandula angustifolia* 'Munstead' has dark blue flowers, underscored by tiny *Viola* 'Jeannie Bellew' covered with creamy-yellow flowers. The plant mass in the centre is dark violet *Salvia* x *superba* 'Ostfriesland' and left of these is a group of low lavender-blue *Geranium wlassovianum* leading round to several *Nepeta racemosa* 'Walker's Low', with hazy mauve-blue flowers. Behind is the violet-red, reedy-leaved *Hemerocallis* 'Summer Wine'. The grey-leaved *Teucrium fruticans* 'Compactum', with light blue flowers, sits between two tall clumps of *Iris* 'Winner's Circle', dark blue with grey foliage. Clumps of *Agapanthus* 'Blue Giant' line the outer edge. An unexpected swathe of lemony *Anthemis tinctoria* 'Wargrave', dotted with burgundy-coloured *Allium sphaerocephalon*, prevents the blue-based border being too bland.

manipulating space

As we have seen (under Colour and Distance, page 130), distance greatly affects the appearance of colours. But often the smaller garden can be enhanced by using colour to create an illusion of greater depth. Beware of choosing to plant bold, brilliant colours like red, orange and yellow on the boundary, as these colours appear to advance and expand and would make the garden appear smaller. Keep the hot colours for closer to the house, and if you wish to echo them elsewhere, use deeper tones like ochre or brown. For the far beds choose blues and paler-toned colours that recede and will increase the garden's apparent depth. Light blues could be echoed closer to by brighter blues and strong magentas. Red can even be appropriate for a boundary if you choose the bluer crimsons and perhaps mix them with violet, mauve, lilac and purple flowers to maintain the illusion of distance. Dark colours tend to retreat, so the dark green shrub *Viburnum tinus* would appear further from us than would the bright green *Griselinia littoralis*, planted in the same place.

A bonus of small spaces is that, seen close to, all colours are sharper and more intense. Contrast is also at its strongest close up, both in value and tone, and detail also becomes more noticeable. So near the house, the blocks of colour used can be far smaller than in the larger garden but will still be more richly contrasting. The numbers in a planting group may be reduced to three or five, so that intricate plants like eryngiums can be enjoyed in this way. Colour contrasts may be exploited here, for example by planting yellow *Lysimachia punctata* beside magenta *Geranium psilostemon*. Further away, the bluer notes of the geranium would be lost and the lysimachia would dominate, but close up, the contrast becomes much richer as well as the flower detail more visible. Alternatively, you might try planting glowing amber-yellow *Coreopsis grandiflora* 'Mayfield Giant' among deep velvet-red *Cosmos atrosanguineus*, treating both as annuals.

Further away from the house, intricacy could give way to larger herbaceous 'sweeps' to avoid a fussy look. Try to curb your instinct

to create a horticultural museum, a garden 'dotted' with single plants, which is never easy on the eye.

the numbers game

When seen close to, sharp colour definitions remain true, so blocks of bright colour work best if planted in smaller swatches to exploit the rich contrasts. Groups of three, five and seven have a natural informality that we find pleasing. The main reason for choosing odd numbers is that our sense of logic means that we tend to split even numbers into equal divisions, which is useful in formal situations but otherwise looks unnatural. Many plants lend themselves to being grown in clusters, particularly those that are not substantial enough to go solo, like the aquilegias, compared with the huge silvery cardoons that focus all attention as soloists. Most herbaceous perennials in fact look better planted in groups. Think of the bearded iris cultivars whose exquisite colour combinations are so well displayed in small groups.

Clump-forming plants with lovely foliage, like peonies or poppies, are also better in groups of odd numbers, possibly fringed by neutrally coloured cream or white anthemis. Erect perennials like delphiniums, verbascums and kniphofias also need to be managed as a numbered fraternity of individuals. But there are some plants — like thalictrums, phlox, heleniums and asters — that are improved by being seen as a drifting mass rather than as groups or individuals. Other plants can be woven in as a slim, flowing band of colour: hemerocallis and achilleas would be effective used in this way. To add a finishing touch to a planting, allow smaller speckles of colour to infiltrate in the form of plants like scabious and alliums.

above: **In such an intimate enclosure, the magentas, lilacs and blues have been chosen for their links. Pink tanacetum and phlox with blue campanulas and salvias foster the tranquil mood echoed by cool pink and blue container plants.**

left: **Bronze *Phormium tenax* 'Nanum Purpureum', magenta *Geranium psilostemon* and cerise *Lychnis coronaria* blend tonally and by colour.**

subtle colours

Subtle colours, like dainty form and fine texture, are lost in larger spaces. Only in smaller gardens can we really appreciate delicately pretty flowers like those of the shrub *Gillenia trifoliata*; they 'touch down' like butterflies, appearing just as transient. And the tiny shivering umbels of *Astrantia maxima*, emerging from a papery collar of green-white bracts, cannot be appreciated at a distance, whereas their subtle shades of colour, even in the reddened forms like *A. major* 'Hadspen Blood', are greatly enjoyed close to. The flowers of epimediums are small and fragile-looking but this tough herbaceous plant has good, lasting foliage that makes it a charming ground cover, especially for shade. *Epimedium x versicolor* 'Sulphureum' has tiny cream flowers which are revealed once the leaves have been shorn early in the year. All such plants can easily be lost in a crowd of more flamboyant hues.

So the smaller scale gives gardeners a chance to celebrate detail and to include some of the 'pointilliste' flowers that depend for effect on their many small flowerheads held well above ground. These herbaceous plants are of great value inserted among a heavier flowering mass; they include lilac-blue *Verbena bonariensis*, wine-red *Knautia macedonica*, strident orange *Geum coccineum* and dark red *Potentilla* 'Etna', all of which have simple, non-insistent foliage. Encourage these dots of colour to mingle among other perennials in a random manner, rather like naturalized bulbs, some in groups, others double or single, as they 'happen to fall'.

intoxicating colours

While many gardeners want to play safe, always choosing the more harmonious combinations, others are brave enough to experiment with the jazzy, exciting colours of contrast and clash. It all depends on the mood you wish your garden to have. To exploit the hot-spirited colours in a small garden, plant some purple-red shrubs at the back, like *Berberis thunbergii* 'Red Chief', which grows to 2m (6ft) and spreads wider. Beside it the greyish-purple leaves of *Rosa glauca*, growing to the same height, would be a very pleasing match, or, to add an even darker note for contrast, try sepia *Viburnum sargentii* 'Onondaga', a taller and wider shrub, with foliage that turns deep green and ultimately red-purple by autumn.

Together these would provide a dark mass against which red and amber-coloured herbaceous flowers, peppered with deep midnight-blue, could provide glamour in summer. Consider two or three clumps of *Lupinus* 'Cherry Belle' and *L.* 'Corn Gold' with the dark red, lily-flowered *Hemerocallis* 'Stafford' that has golden centres. Near them, place some spiky flame-orange *Crocosmia*

'Jupiter'. A couple of groups of *Lychnis x arkwrightii* would also be an asset, not only for its brilliant scarlet flowers but also its purple foliage to echo the berberis. *Achillea* 'Terracotta' would bring the colours together and you could weave in a flow of tangerine *Hemerocallis* 'Mauna Loa' and *H.* 'Ruffled Apricot' to lighten the scheme and scatter in the red dots of *Potentilla* 'Gibson's Scarlet'.

For spiky accents, plant separate clumps of small *Phormium* 'Bronze Baby' to contribute drama, or include areas of indigo *Veronica longifolia* 'Foerster's Blue', followed by the hooded inky-purple *Aconitum henryi* 'Spark's Variety'. You might introduce some contrasting cool pinks for early summer with clumping *Iris sibirica* 'Sparkling Rose', which has a slightly mauve tinge. And to brighten the scheme later on, plant several areas of very pale yellow, airy *Nepeta govaniana*, with a border trim of small, cream-coloured *Achillea x lewisii* 'King Edward' to last all summer.

bedded enclosures

The beauty of a large garden is that different areas may be separated off so that the owner can indulge in any colour scheme within them, perhaps screening off a herb garden, a secret garden or a walled one. Average-sized gardens may yet be large enough to section off small areas for specific purposes and these can be kept in order by enclosing them with clipped box for a year-round effect. Dwarf clipped lavender or *Santolina chamaecyparissus* could be used to make silver-grey hedges in place of the usual green box or, for a more informal look, try an edging of grassy green chives (*Allium schoenoprasum*), with purple flowers in spring. The resulting patterns offer a chance to explore temporary colour effects with spring bulbs and bedding annuals. Think of velvety orange and red wallflowers or antirrhinums, dotted with tall pink tulips. Later in spring, a protected area could be filled with the rainbow colours of tender peony-flowered mixed buttercups (*Ranunculus asiaticus* Turban Group) and for high summer the cool reds and pinks of mixed sweet william (*Dianthus barbatus*), framed by lilac-blue ageratums and infiltrated with powder-blue love-in-a-mist (*Nigella damascena*).

opposite above: **Subtle fresh greens can be enjoyed in an intimate dark space. The fern *Asplenium scolopendrium*, with its glossy, light-reflecting leaves is planted with arching Solomon's seal (*Polygonatum multiflorum*), both growing from a sea of carpeting *Soleirolia soleirolii*.**

opposite below: **In close-up detail, red orach (*Atriplex hortensis* 'Rubra') mingles with *Penstemon* 'Port Wine', silvery *Artemisia absinthium* and chocolate-coloured annual cornflowers (*Centaurea cyanus* 'Black Ball'). Around them, *Clematis* 'Niobe' rambles at will.**

In town the demands on an enclosed, often hard-surfaced and lawn-less garden are special. By their nature, courtyards are unlikely to have beautiful views so they often become inward-looking, screening off the urban surroundings and giving a sense of privacy. The other feature of a constricted urban space is that the walls often offer more growing opportunities than the floor, so climbing plants are key ingredients. There are clematis, vines, roses and 'exotic' tender climbers, as well as many pleasing annual climbers to choose from, making the choice of colour almost limitless.

The main constraint in an urban courtyard is likely to be its size, so your aim may be to create a feeling of spaciousness. A reliable way of doing this is to use light blue or pale turquoise colours that appear to recede, against the 'backdrop' walls, avoiding those hot colours, like red or strong orange, that advance. Pale yellows, cream and apricot tones will help to foster an illusion of increased depth too. Relaxing colours, these will add a tranquil quality to the enclosed space.

above: **This unusual container grouping in glazed pots is based on red flowers and foliage. Included are: *Heuchera micrantha* var. *diversifolia* 'Palace Purple', *Dianthus* 'Diamond Scarlet', phormiums and cyclamen.**

right: **A tiled terrace in a small courtyard has a central gravelled bed for an apple tree and small campanulas and geraniums. Beds fringed with *Alchemilla mollis*, perennials and shrubs surround this sunken area.**

greening the boundaries

Some all-year-round evergreens will conceal the boundaries – even if they need judicious pruning to keep them within bounds. Look at the plants suggested under Unity (see page 103); in addition, here are some suggestions for smaller shrubs to suit the scale of the urban courtyard. Dark green *Viburnum tinus* 'Eve Price' grows to 3m (10ft) but can be pruned, while bottle-green *Prunus laurocerasus* Low 'n' Green is only 75cm (2ft 6in) tall and the pale green *Pittosporum tenuifolium* 'Irene Paterson' a compact 1.2m (4ft). For the brighter lime greens, look to another pittosporum, *P. tenuifolium* 'Warnham Gold', or the fragrant deciduous *Philadelphus coronarius* 'Aurea', that is golden yellow in sun but grows better out of it because of leaf burn, making it a lime-green colour.

Some well-textured bright green plants for sun include hazy fennel (*Foeniculum vulgare*), a tall perennial that sets off yellow or orange flowers beautifully, and the cool silver-green *Melianthus major* that is lovely with cool pink, blue or plum-coloured flowers. In a shaded area, try growing some frondy ferns, with their decorative patterns, below shrubs with polished leaves, such as aucubas.

There are plants with green flowers – like some euphorbias – that thrive in a warm, protected environment. You could try statuesque evergreen *Euphorbia characias* subsp. *wulfenii* 'John Tomlinson'; though this shrub is 1.2m (4ft) in diameter, I do feel that compact spaces need some large statements. If all the plants were small the effect would be rather coy. Another large shrub, a fig (*Ficus carica* 'Brown Turkey'), can be grown against a sunny wall and trained flat. If the roots are restricted it will be a smaller plant but the deciduous, stylish palmate dove-grey to green leaves are still large and turn yellow in autumn. For shade, another spurge, the spreading *Euphorbia amygdaloides* var. *robbiae*, is a great standby for the most difficult situations, with lime-green flowers and dark green foliage; you will need to cut back the rhizomes if it spreads too far. Oriental hellebores and unusual *Paris polyphylla* are shapely shade-loving plants for spring and summer. In a sunnier part of the courtyard you could pick up on the green theme with spikes of greenish-yellow *Kniphofia* 'Percy's Pride', trimmed at ground level with a few jade-green rosette-leaved *Heuchera* 'Mint Frost'.

luminous colours

The enclosed town garden can be almost as important at night as it is in the day. Indeed, in some months the owner may not see the garden in daylight except at the weekends when, if the curtains are open all winter, the courtyard becomes part of the indoor experience. And on a summer evening, dining outside may be *de rigueur*. So while colours that are dark will be unnoticed for a lot of the time, the luminous whites and pastels and their ghostly 'lack' of colour is worth exploring.

opposite: **In a contemporary garden, tiered ornamental grasses are planted in a raised bed retained by galvanized metal sheeting:** *Miscanthus sinensis,* **at the back, then** *Miscanthus sinensis* **'Variegatus' are fronted by small variegated carex, blue festucas and golden carex. They will have to be thinned as they mature.**

above: **Green dominates in an urban garden on two levels designed by the author. The tall bamboo that reaches to the next level and the domed clipped box in containers links the two courtyards together.**

For the night garden, always aim to include some light-reflecting flowers and foliage among the rest of the planting. Consider geraniums, in white, pale blue and pink forms, as they will flower for much of the summer, as well as small bulbous anemones for spring and tall herbaceous ones for late summer. Early in the year, white dicentras, narcissi and tulips, followed by lilies, will still be seen as the last of the light fades. For later in summer you might choose pale blue scabious, salvias and agapanthus with cream anthemis, achillea and irises to draw the eye in twilight. For shade, include some shrubs with variegated leaves, like evergreen *Euonymus fortunei* 'Emerald Gaiety' and the taller deciduous *Philadelphus coronarius* 'Variegatus', a lovely slow grower, as well as evergreen *Rhamnus alaternus* 'Argenteovariegata', an excellent shrub to light up semi-shade. *Iris foetidissima* 'Variegata' will be luminous even in deep shade, as will pale blue-leaved or variegated hostas or a particularly attractive lily-of-the-valley, *Convallaria majalis* 'Albostriata'. In sunnier areas, consider a different iris, the white-striped fanning *Iris pallida* 'Variegata', or *Sisyrinchium striatum* 'Aunt May'.

sun colours

To bring sunlight to an urban space, use yellow-bright flowers and foliage. In spring the fresh yellow grass *Milium effusum* 'Aureum' can be echoed with the star-shaped flowers of early-flowering daylilies (*Hemerocallis dumortieri*). Follow these with the neat form of lemon-yellow *Anthemis tinctoria* 'Wargrave', overlapping in summer with mounds of golden-yellow *Coreopsis verticillata* 'Grandiflora', in which daisy flowers nestle in fine moss-green foliage. By late summer there will still be colour on the lime-silver *Helichrysum* 'Sulphur Light'. For other brightly hued flowers, look at the suggestions given under Vivacious Energy (page 50).

Include with these yellow flowers some in light blue, white and cream (see A Mood of Calm, page 42), to maintain the light-giving nature of the planting scheme, and perhaps add in a little apricot for warmth. Try forms of iris like amber *Iris* 'Ultimatum', deeper orange *I.* 'Tanzanian Tangerine' and the smaller, richer-hued *I.* 'Gingerbread Man'. Later in the season you could consider tall *Crocosmia* 'Jupiter' and some chrysanthemums for their warm copper-orange tones.

You may of course prefer more intense and dramatic plants, in which case you could look at the exotic type of planting described later in this chapter (see page 170). Or the interior colours of the house may influence the choices out of doors; often the city garden has to reflect the sophistication or colourful character of the building itself. The white-garden plants suggested on page 106 may be appropriate here. While in theory any colour theme is suitable for a courtyard, everything depends on the quality of the light. If you live in a sunny climate and the yard is very hot in summer, think about some of the silver-leaved plants described on page 166.

wall shrubs and climbers

Where the boundaries are high but the enclosed space very limited, climbing plants are generally more suitable than wall shrubs, except for those that can be easily pruned to lie flat, like chaenomeles, pyracantha and escallonia. The deciduous deutzias also make good background shrubs for early summer. Mostly white-flowered, there are other colours like fragrant, deep pink *Deutzia* x *elegantissima* 'Rosealind'. For bold colours there is the slightly tender evergreen shrub *Leptospermum scoparium* 'Red Damask', with small red flowers, as well as blue-flowered ceanothus in different forms. Do not let a season go by without pruning these shrubs to control their size, or they will quickly outgrow their space and become top-heavy.

clematis

Of all climbers, clematis are the most rewarding in really small gardens, provided the roots are shaded and in deep, rich soil that never dries out. They take up very little room and yet offer a vast

choice of colour, foliage and season so that you can have one in flower almost throughout the year.

In a clematis-based planting scheme for a wall, I would include one evergreen climber as well, say *Trachelospermum jasminoides*, which is white-flowered, scented and not too vigorous. The small nodding early blue flowers of *Clematis alpina* 'Columbine' or 'Frances Rivis' would be invaluable to start the season, which is so important to cheer us in a town garden. *Clematis macropetala* is similar – look for 'Markham's Pink'. Neither of these species have the huge 'dinner plate' flowers but are delicate in structure and in colour. Consider raspberry-pink *C.* 'Carnaby' for early and late summer, because it will flower in shade. But for sunny walls you could try *C.* 'Royal Velvet' for its summer-long rich burgundy-purple blooms with red stamens and *C. viticella* 'Polish Spirit', which is a blue-purple with creamy stamens that also lasts through summer. A delicate papery white would lighten the scheme and *C. viticella* 'Alba Luxurians' is an extremely pretty and reliable form. The evergreen *Clematis cirrhosa* var. *balearica* flowers from late autumn to early spring, with delicate cream flowers; a form named 'Freckles' displays hanging creamy bellflowers among the ferny foliage.

Though there will probably be little space for planting at the foot of clematis, there are some smaller plants that will hide their thin, leggy look. Consider small heucheras like *Heuchera* 'Red Spangles' or *H.* 'Snow Storm', with mottled leaves and pink flowers. Many geraniums have good foliage, like the long-flowering blue *Geranium* 'Rozanne' or the very low-growing, pale pink *G. cinereum* 'Apple Blossom'. Otherwise look for well-foliaged plants that would also shade the clematis roots, as well as offer flowers. Smaller daylilies, like *Hemerocallis* 'Summer Wine', or larger lemon-yellow *Anthemis tinctoria* 'E.C. Buxton', with parsley-like foliage, are good contenders.

climbing roses

The many choices for an enclosed urban garden must include the climbing roses. While ramblers usually flower magnificently only once

top: **Trachelospermum jasminoides, with its star-shaped flowers, is glorious against the blue agapanthus heads.**

above: **'Madame Caroline Testout' is an ideal climbing rose for a trellis-covered boundary. Beside it is an early-flowering clematis and, below,** *Rhamnus alaternus* **'Argenteovariegata' with the buff-pink heuchera flowers.**

right: **Yellows dominate a container group, with bidens and petunias, but grey sempervivums settle the scheme.**

and tend to be vigorous, climbing roses may flower through the summer or have two wonderful periods of excess. The choices are almost as limitless as clematis and a good catalogue will help you decide on colour. There are hot colours, dark ones, pastels and bi-colours. Those with strong colour include deep red *Rosa* Sympathie, crimson, fragrant *R.* 'Etoile de Hollande', apricot *R.* 'Meg', orange-yellow *R.* 'Maigold' and pretty pink-and-white *R.* Handel. Look also for size, period of flowering, type of flower – single or clustered – and disease resistance. Aspect is important: some will cope with north- or east-facing boundaries, like flaming *R.* Danse du Feu, golden *R.* 'Gloire de Dijon', deep red *R.* 'Guinée' and strong pink, fragrant *R.* 'Zéphirine Drouhin', although all would perform even better in a sunnier spot.

other climbing plants

Other hardy climbers suited to the urban scene include fragrant, white-flowered evergreen *Trachelospermum jasminoides*, the china-blue summer-flowering *Solanum crispum* 'Glasnevin' or the slightly less hardy and less vigorous white form, *S. jasminoides* 'Album'. I would avoid most honeysuckles because, although pretty and scented, they are plants that grow with careless abandon, which is lovely in a country garden but a tangled mess in town.

LIGHT-REFLECTING SCHEME

The focus of this enclosed courtyard is the small soft-grey leaved, blossoming and fruiting tree *Sorbus vilmorinii*. Beneath it cream *Aconitum* 'Ivorine', fronted by dwarf *Iris* 'Blue Line', are planted next to soft blue *Geranium himalayense* 'Irish Blue', echoed by the smaller, brighter blue *G.* 'Little Gem', which follows the rounded form of pink-mauve winter-flowering *Daphne* x *burkwoodii* 'Somerset'. On the wall behind, claret-coloured *Clematis* 'Niobe' is echoed around the garden by dots of *Knautia macedonica*. On the furthest boundary wall, evergreen blue-flowering *Ceanothus burkwoodii* is fronted by pale yellow *Hemerocallis* 'Towhead' and, to its left, *Cistus* 'Silver Pink', with blue *Campanula persicifolia* 'Telham Beauty' to the right.

Trachelospermum jasminoides covers the left-hand wall with grey-leaved, blue *Iris* 'Impetuous' in front. Small *Viola cornuta* 'Letitia' edges the bed with its pretty rose-lilac flowers and it ends with the low moss-green *Santolina virens* 'Primrose Gem', covered with yellow button flowers.

Colour choices will be influenced by where the garden is — its latitude and aspect — as well as by the climatic conditions and the nature of the surroundings, from countryside to domestic suburbs to inner city. There is also the consideration of light — whether the garden is exposed to full sunlight at midday or receives mostly morning or evening light — and how shaded it is. The closer gardens are to the equator, the more intense the contrast of shadow with bright searching light. Colours can be chosen to work effectively with all conditions as well as, sometimes, resolving problems.

The properties of light, shade and contrast are all part of the fascination of the art of gardening. As we have seen, light alters everything. Early morning and early evening are the best times to take photographs, when shadows are long and light does not blaze down from on high, flattening volume and concealing detail. By midday, when the sun is overhead, the light is unforgivingly glaring and it reduces the impact of colour. Shadows at this time are small and insignificant, removing all three-dimensional properties of form, texture and depth, as well as colour.

right: **Evening light makes these flowers glow with richer colour. Sharing a need for full sun and well-drained gritty soil, silvery *Stachys byzantina*, annual dark red orach and spires of white *Verbascum chaixii* surround the golden cup flowers of *Oenothera fruticosa* 'Fireworks', with brown-purple tinged leaves.**

soft blue light

In temperate zones the diffuse quality of light means that shadows are neither sharp nor soot-black but more a gentle chiaroscuro of reflected light. The associated building materials are most likely to be the neutral colours of stone, earthy browns and ochres or brick-reds, rather than the boldly coloured rendered concrete or sharp whites found in hotter climates. And the colours of naturally indigenous plants will on the whole be softer than those of the sub-tropical divas.

In these temperate gardens, where the air is virtually colour-washed with the blue light of damper climes, stridency is best avoided in favour of gentle harmony. Many modern hybrids have been bred regardless of subtlety, because flagrant colour can be impressive – and it sells well. But the more excitable colours and combinations are too intrusive for these latitudes. Flower colours that flatter each other in such circumstances are those that are familiar from the 'romantic' tradition of flower gardens: hues that include pink, lilac, powder-blue, deep blue, cream, wine-red, crimson, clear yellow, lemon-yellow, and a mix of silvers and fresh greens. These colours are more evocative of enchantment than of energy and the plants characteristically mingle in tranquil accord rather than sweeping or forming clumps. All the combinations suggested are for gardens that are sunlit.

right: Overtones of blue affect the intensity of maroon *Hemerocallis* 'Summer Wine' and rich plum-red *Astrantia major* 'Hadspen Blood', with the pewter-grey foliage of *Rosa glauca* a sympathetic foil.

Climbing plants such as roses, clematis and honeysuckles are traditionally in the forefront of romantic gardens, surrounded by the pastel colours of hazy nepetas, grey and blue lavenders, geraniums and pinks, with fulsome blue campanulas, cool, voluptuous phlox, daisy-like cream anthemis, fluffy thalictrums, papery poppies, self-seeding diascias and spreads of *Alchemilla mollis*. But such light, delicate planting schemes need careful thought if the result is not to be too anaemic. The rinsed-out hues described benefit from the insertion of some darker contrasts, like indigo salvias or purple delphiniums, or you could warm the overall blue note with rust-coloured daylilies or irises. Some dark flower colours will add finesse to the romantic garden, which is where the purples of aconitum and geranium come in, while maroon *Knautia macedonica, Cosmos atrosanguineus, Allium sphaerocephalon, Penstemon* 'Raven' and *Cirsium rivulare* will add depth as well as contrast.

shrubs

Always important in the structure of planting schemes, shrubs can provide form among the luxuriance. The flowering shrubs most appropriate here would include mounds of cistus, like the neat *Cistus corbariensis* with pink buds that open to many small white

above left: **Misted artificially, this small garden relies on foliage for its colour. Lime- and grass-green ornamental grasses with small, rounded whipcord hebes, purple heucheras and blue spreading junipers surround the bright butter-yellow leaves of the beautiful** *Acer shirasawanum* **'Aureum'.**

above centre: **The foliage of bronze fennel sets off the glowing orange flowers of** *Hieraceum aurantiacum,* **with the softer apricot colours of poppies, daylilies and foxgloves blending into the distance.**

above right: **Seen against the fresh green of spring are cool-coloured lily tulips, including maroon** *Tulipa* **'Burgundy' and white-edged pink** *T.* **'Ballade'.**

opposite above: **The greyed-pink 'old rose' colour of** *Papaver orientale* **'Patty's Plum' makes it an ideal associate for roses.**

opposite below: **Clipped box adds formal structure to a lush, romantic planting scheme in which pink and white roses dominate, with grey-leaved** *Lychnis coronaria* **'Alba' massed at their feet.**

A ROMANTIC ROSE GARDEN

This essentially romantic garden has all the classic components of the 'English' style: green lawns, a wisteria-clad pergola and many roses with scented companion planting. The two areas are separated by dark yew hedging and the left side is more shaded. The first garden, entered between two evergeen *Viburnum davidii*, has a circular lawn. Two fragrant flowering shrubs on the sunny side are white *Philadelphus* 'Belle Etoile' and deep purple *Syringa* 'Katherine Havermayer' with several hybrid musk cream-pink *Rosa* 'Penelope' between them. On the opposite side two *Buddleja davidii* 'Black Knight' echo the dark purple, next to *Viburnum tinus* 'Gwenllian' and, further along, the yellow winter-flowering *Mahonia* x *media* 'Charity'. In front are five pure white *Rosa* Iceberg, then several pink-yellow English roses, *R.* Abraham Derby. The glorious yellow rose *R.* Graham Thomas can be seen by the yew hedge. Blue *Nepeta sibirica* 'Souvenir d'André Chaudron', dark blue *Aconitum carmichaelii*, grey-leaved *Perovskia* 'Filligran' and two areas of magenta-purple *Lavandula stoechas* create links, with the reedy, white-flowering *Libertia grandiflora* encircling the lawn. Leaving the first garden between two white-flowering evergreen *Choisya ternata* one enters the second, rectangular area, the lawn edged with box hedging. Dominant trees are the great white cherry (*Prunus* 'Taihaku') and two corner-sited small trees, a small silver-grey-leaved weeping pear (*Pyrus salicifolia* 'Pendula') and a lilac (*Syringa* 'Bellicent') with scented dark rose flowers. Mixed evergreen hedging encloses the garden, made up of blue holly (*Ilex* x *meserveae* 'Blue Princess') on the shady side and *Escallonia* 'Slieve Donard' facing the sun. Beside the pear, in sun, are several salmon-pink bush roses, *Rosa* 'Paul Shirville'. Along the far end are pink *R.* Bonica and soft pink *R.* 'Savoy Hotel', leading to the corner where *Rosa* William Shakespeare produces deep crimson double flowers. Again, blue flowers link thoughout, with light blue *Geranium pratense* 'Mrs Kendall Clark' and violet-blue *Campanula lactiflora* 'Prichard's Variety'. Frothy lime-green *Alchemilla mollis* and three tall *Acanthus spinosus* do well on the more shaded side of the garden.

above: **A rich pink centifolia rose has** *Clematis viticella* **'Kermasina' as a rambling associate, with a mass of** *Geranium endressii* **below.**

flowers and the taller, aromatic-leaved *C. ladanifer*, whose larger white flowers have golden eyes. Shrubby potentillas tend to be round in form, although there are some low spreaders too. There are pink, white, apricot and red colours but a great favourite of mine is an old one, *Potentilla fruticosa* 'Primrose Beauty', that fits in with nearly all colour schemes. You might choose the more rigid hebes or fastigiate pale blue rosemary as accents.

Other shrubs may have a less disciplined form that fulfils the romantic nature of the garden, like many of the wedding-white philadelphus. Consider also small lilacs, such as scented lavender-mauve *Syringa microphylla*, large, fluffy-flowered *Ceanothus* 'Autumnal Blue', arching buddlejas in blue, purple, lilac and white, lush-foliaged tree peonies and lemon-yellow tree lupins.

roses

Rose gardens are admired everywhere and today roses offer almost any colour and can be easy to grow if their requirements are understood. The rose needs full sun but no temperature extremes, so cool climates with reliable moisture and a mild atmosphere are ideal. There are many different kinds of rose, from very tall shrubs like *Rosa* 'Frühlingsmorgen', a light yellow modern shrub that may reach 2–2.2m (6–7ft), to the miniature 'patio' roses.

Species roses have soft, more 'natural' colouring and often pretty foliage that is sometimes greyish, like pink-flowered *R. glauca*, or the tall thorny, white-flowered *R. fedtschenkoana*. They fit into wild plantings, when used with dogwoods and elders, or make lovely associations within a mixed border, adding height and substance, and with flower colours that merge into almost any scheme. By the end of summer masses of red and orange hips among yellowing foliage revitalize the tired border. Some may be over 3m (10ft) tall, like *R. moyesii*, a ferny-leaved species with small blood-red flowers that appear only once but are followed by magnificent scarlet bottle-shaped hips. In addition there are hybridized forms like blush-pink *R. pimpinellifolia* 'Stanwell Perpetual' that may repeat bloom.

Shrub roses tend to be densely leaved and make a good shape that enables them to fit in anywhere, unlike the hybrid teas that look

awkwardly undressed below. These tend to branch out stiffly, with heavy foliage, but the great virtues of these hybrids is that they have large, beautifully structured flowers in exquisite colours and they bloom for months – added to which they are blessed with vigour and disease resistance. Merging the best characteristics of the old with the new has resulted in the English rose, sharing qualities with old roses, like the gallicas and damasks, but being consistently in flower, fragrant and rarely succumbing to mildew and black spot.

Cool colours such as cold pink, crimson-red and white are characteristic of the old shrub roses, many of which are hybridized, like the pink hybrid musk *R.* 'Felicia', the white rugosa *R.* 'Schneezwerg' and the highly fragrant, velvety crimson *R.* William Shakespeare. There are also some attractive warm-toned yellows, coppers and apricot shades such as the yolk-yellow double *R.* Graham Thomas, the hybrid musk *R.* 'Cornelia' and the pale apricot-pink *R.* 'Penelope'. The warm and cold colours are best grown in separate areas since neither flatters the other.

If you prefer sprays of flowers on a stem to single- or double-flowered roses, look to the floribundas. These are more informal in habit, creating a mass effect of colour, so they grow very well with plants like nepeta, spreading geraniums and *Alchemilla mollis*. There is the charming *R.* 'English Miss', light pink with a warm heart, coppery, semi-double fragrant apricot *R.* 'Southampton' and *R.* Iceberg, a continuous-flowering white. Always check the eventual height and habit of a rose because many are large and some sprawl. A neat accompaniment like maroon, rose or ivory-coloured small bearded irises, soft lilac *Erysimum* 'Bowles' Mauve' or deep blue *Salvia nemorosa* 'Ostfriesland' would flatter such rose colours.

The most famous hybrid tea, *R.* Peace says it all for single-flowered roses. Although the form is stiff, the leaves are glossy dark green and the beautifully structured flowers are light yellow flushed pink. Surround it with French lavender, reddish-purple *Lavandula stoechas*, or a trim of deeply coloured violas for a contrast without taking anything from the shrub. Another rose predicted to have a long future is *R.* Silver Jubilee, its classically formed flowers peach-pink, with luminous overtones of gold and cream. Its lush-foliaged habit would be flattered by association with lilac-blue *Lavandula angustifolia* 'Hidcote' or compact *Geranium* 'Rozanne'.

Many of the English roses are doubles, so the colours are intensified. Roses that are deeply coloured are crucial in a romantic scheme to prevent an over-sweet sentimentality. Look for the saturated colour of *R.* 'Charles de Mills', a gallica densely packed with wine-crimson petals that age to a dusky purple, or the richly perfumed repeat-flowering *R.* 'Souvenir du Docteur Jamain', another claret-coloured rose. Both look wonderful with really dark blues like indigo-black *Iris* 'Superstition' followed later in summer by *Salvia x superba* 'Mainacht' and smaller, purple-blue *Geranium magnificum*.

When planting roses, many of the herbaceous perennials so far suggested make well-tried associates. If the area were large I would add phlox, lilies, daylilies and anthemis. Many of these will shade the roots, which suits roses well. Plan the colours on the same principles as the schemes described and, for fun, add some sparks like tiger lilies with orange or wine-red roses, transparent tall lilac-blue *Verbena bonariensis* in front of apricot, yellow and cream roses, or ornamental grasses like a mass of hazy, buff-coloured stipas to contrast with the more strongly coloured, densely leaved hybrid tea roses. On a smaller scale, low-growing 'patio' roses, like pink *R.* Queen Mother, apricot *R.* Sweet Dream and white pompon flowered *R.* Bianco, can be fitted in, with lush flowers and scent.

flowers in the mixed border

Merging shrubs with herbaceous perennials can extend the flowering season and create the full glory of what is often described as the English style. An evergreen framework creates secluded spaces and flowering shrubs may be kept on the perimeter or mixed in with general planting around the garden. A sense of homogeneity is crucial if the garden is to hang together. So if the garden is romantic in style and the light is cool and blue, the planting will be enhanced if it is backed with green foliage. Leaves may be grassy green, like hemerocallis, or darker, like those of leucanthemums. Some, like those of *Coreopsis verticillata* and fennel, will be hazy emerald-green, some elegantly divided like the fresh green foliage of lupins. Other leaf colours may be silver or bluish, like artemisias, stachys and grassy *Elymus magellanicus*. If you wish, a few really strong colours can be chosen, like the flattering brownish leaves of cimicifuga or the purple of heuchera: balance these by repeating them around the site.

Colour associations are not enough if there is no contrast of form or subtlety of shape. So consider inserting some solid masses in small groups, like peonies, poppies, fuchsias, spiraea, lavatera and shrub potentillas. Include the odd single statement like *Cynara cardunculus, Melianthus major, Acanthus spinosus, Euphorbia characias,* damp-loving *Rheum palmatum* and *Rodgersia aesculifolia*, as well as late-summer *Eupatorium purpureum*, to suggest the volume of shrubs.

Provided there are some distinctive outlines, the main planting can afford to be less shapely and could include salvias, daylilies, geraniums, penstemons, thalictrum, asters, campanulas, phlox and verbenas. Among these, the punctuation of dramatic spears will provide essential contrast: choose from delphiniums, foxgloves, veronicastrum, sidalcea, kniphofia, lythrum and lupins. Tall persicaria adds rhythm, with its warm, deep red poker flowers.

opposite: **Soft pink *Rosa* 'Albertine' and pale blue delphiniums make a romantic partnership.**

right: **Romantic blued light and fresh greens make gentle associates for deep pink *Rosa mutabilis*, pink penstemons, luminous pale lilac-pink *Salvia farinacea*, light blue perovskia with grey leaves, and the silvery *Artemisia ludoviciana* 'Valerie Finnis'. But dark plum filbert leaves at the back and the sharp grey phormium foliage, plus the maroon dots of *Allium sphaerocephalon*, make contrasts that energize the overall effect.**

woodland shade

The shady garden holds great charm for some gardeners and I confess to a real affection for woodland, provided the shade is not too dense and there are clearings, or glades, creating opportunities to grow more highly coloured flowers in better light conditions. In the sun-filled gardens described previously, areas of shade make an invaluable contrast and are a relief in brightly lit conditions, providing alternative space for sitting as well as a chance to grow a different style of shade-loving planting.

The character of natural woodland is established by the deeply recessive dark greens that provide a foil for luminously pale colours, with dappled light and glades offering some stronger colour opportunities. Some tree canopies are denser than others and in traditional old woodland, trees like horse chestnuts create dark depths. In a garden situation you may occasionally need to have the crowns of certain trees lifted to let in some light, but if you are planting trees you could choose those that filter light rather than suppress it. Mountain ash, like varieties of *Sorbus aucuparia*, and silver birch such as *Betula pendula* 'Tristis' have relatively small leaves that move in the breeze and allow dappled light through. Beech trees are densely canopied. In summer they mean dry soil, which is why you will see bare ground in a beech wood. You should avoid limes because of the sticky honeydew that drops from them and be aware that large leaves, like those of sycamores, blanket rather than carpet the ground in autumn. Beware too of the shallow roots of trees like flowering cherry that are surface rooters. These and birch will impoverish the soil by shallow rooting, so good preparation is essential, with the addition of plenty of well-rotted organic matter.

left: **Spring in this woodland garden looks wonderful, swept with varieties of *Helleborus orientalis* whose flowers are characteristically green-white, rose-pink, deep purple and green with dark red freckles.**

left: **In damp shade the pink, peach, lilac and mauve pastel colours of candelabra primulas are intoxicating.**

opposite: **A mass of pale green** Tiarella cordifolia **with cream flowers thrives as ground cover in lightly shaded woodland beside fans of the damp-loving shuttlecock fern** (Matteuccia struthiopteris).

There are some ground-covering plants that will cope with even dense shade, like ivy, deadnettle or periwinkle. Taller carpeting plants like tiarella, tellima and some geraniums will manage too, although none of these offers strong colour. Tiarellas have delicate pale pink flowers and pretty red-marked foliage and *Tellima grandiflora* throws up rows of pale yellow-green flower spikes; the form 'Purpurteppich' has purple foliage and pink-tinged flowers. Pale pink *Geranium endressii* and aromatic *G. macrorrhizum* 'Bevan's Variety', a purple-red, provide soft tints.

There are some lovely North American plants, sparkling with jewel colours early in the year, that revel in woodland conditions. These are all small plants but they add massed pinpoints of colour. Think, for example, of delicate-looking yellow, white and mauve erythroniums and American cowslips (*Dodecatheon meadia*). Or consider pretty yellow *Clintonia borealis*, for neutral and acid soils, as well as blue, purple or pink hepaticas, for neutral or alkaline soils. For acid conditions, consider pink, maroon and yellow trilliums and creeping *Cornus canadensis*, also with white flowers.

If your garden is not very large, a small secret area could be devoted to a mini-woodland where the character beneath, say, a group of silver birches is quickly established with emerald-green ferns. If the land has never been real woodland you will need to incorporate rich compost and leafmould to simulate the natural conditions, which would be dampish. Ideally, trees should begin to leaf in late spring, allowing early spring bulbs to enjoy themselves, but should hold on to their foliage for as long as possible.

spring in woodland

The woodland garden is truly stirring when the fresh greens emerge in spring. Gardens in northern temperate latitudes naturally produce colours that are much softer than those of the rhododendrons. Plants such as wood anemones, pulmonarias, hellebores and bluebells all associate well together close to and English bluebells are superb in the mass seen from a distance. But the pleasures of detail come from some luminous pastels that develop in shade, like primroses, white asperula and blue omphalodes as well as lime-green alchemilla, cream Solomon's seal, grassy variegated luzula and the small white bells of lily-of-the-valley. Lest this is too bland, add in magenta-purple honesty (*Lunaria biennis*) that will seed everywhere, and a mix of foxgloves in different summer colours.

The charisma of hellebores lies in their gently restrained colours and shapely evergreen leaves. Spring is the season for these shade-loving, long-flowering perennials and the choice is well worth studying. The taller, green-flowered *Helleborus argutifolius* (syn. *H. corsicus*) makes a large clump or mass of sculpted leaves from the centre of which apple-green flowers appear in late winter and last for months. *H. foetidus* is slightly smaller, with flower clusters of small, hanging pale green bells, often with a fine edging of maroon, that are also long-lasting. Both are easy to grow in humus-rich woodland and will seed around. They contrast in texture rather than colour with the unfurling pinnate fronds of deep shade-loving ferns like tall *Dryopteris filix-mas* and the more elegant soft shield fern (*Polystichum setiferum*). Smaller hellebores, like hybrids of

H. orientalis, are equally leafy and may be deep plum-purple with creamy stamens, like *H. x hybridus* 'Pluto', to dark crimson speckled with white, like *H. orientalis* subsp. *guttatus*; it has green, cream, light yellow and pink forms too. They could be pleasingly associated with blue, pink or white spreads of tuberous *Anemone blanda*, ferny-leaved dicentras and light yellow *Primula vulgaris*, anticipating spring. For sharper colour contrast, *Ranunculus ficaria* 'Brazen Hussy' is the familiar shining golden celandine but the almost heart-shaped leaves are glossy bronze, setting off the flowers to perfection.

Other ferns add much to woodland planting as the season develops. The smooth, glossy emerald-green hart's tongue fern (*Asplenium scolopendrium*) unfurls to form tall, slim strap leaves. Some forms of the Crispum Group have crimped edges, but they are still shiny and make a good contrast beside more feathery ferns or the hardy evergreen iris (*Iris foetidissima*). This plant has modest blue or cream flowers but is really grown for its smooth sword-shaped leaves with bright orange fruits in winter. If you can do without the fruits, there is a variegated form that is white and green all year through, lighting up the darkest corner. It is slow growing and should have old leaves cut out in spring but is worth the trouble.

More substantial herbaceous foliage comes from clumps of spreading *Symphytum caucasicum* with massed spring flowers that are either pale blue with crimson or cream with pink, as well as the tall blue-flowering *S. x uplandicum* 'Variegatum' that brings light to shady spots. So does *Brunnera macrophylla* 'Hadspen Cream', which surrounds its sprays of light blue flowers with large, heart-shaped, cream-edged leaves. Epimediums have light leaves that float above the ground with either deep pink, yellow or white flowers, seen only if the leaves are cut back in winter. *Epimedium x versicolor* 'Sulphureum' could be effectively backed by finely fronded lady ferns (*Adiantum pedatum*) or *Omphalodes verna* with its intense blue sprays.

woodland with acid soil

The look of woodland when it is gardened rather than natural can result in some amazingly strong colour combinations if you take lime-hating rhododendrons and azaleas into consideration. Rhododendrons tend to be shallow-rooted and prefer their acidic soil to be damp but never waterlogged, and enriched with humus. All rhododendrons need some sun or partial shade so are best planted at the edge of a woodland rather than in dense shadow.

Rhododendrons may be as tall as trees, like the rose-pink 5m (15ft) high deciduous *Rhododendron vaseyi* or the remarkable *R. sinogrande*, a 10m (33ft) high tree whose huge oblong evergreen leaves have a brownish indumentum, like a very fine furry coat, on their undersides. Large lemon-cream flower trusses grace the plant in mid-spring. Where there is more light and if you want compact plants, look at varieties of *R. yakushimanum* – neat, dome-shaped, very free-flowering plants. The colours range widely and include light-yellow-touched-with-salmon 'Grumpy', pink-and-cream 'Percy Wiseman' and vermilion 'Titian Beauty', all ideal for a small garden.

The majority of rhododendrons are cool-hued so that the reds are crimson, like 'Cynthia' and the pinks cold, such as *R.* 'Pink Pearl' with frilly petals; there are mauve colours like *R.* 'Blue Boy', violet-blue, and deep purple, like *R.* 'Purple Splendour', a round shrub of 1.5m (5ft). Some are more hyacinth-blue, like the small *R.* 'Blue Diamond' or the species *R. augustinii* that grows to 2m (6–7ft). There are magnificent white forms, like handsome *R.* 'Sappho', 1.8m (6ft) high with purple buds, and compact green-white 'Palestrina', an evergreen azalea. Among low-key colours white can dominate, so use with discretion.

The colours of hybrid azaleas tend to be much warmer. Most have been bred to produce hot scarlets, oranges, golds and yellows (and some revel in full sunlight, so are not relevant here). Deciduous azaleas can have autumnal colour to rival the acers, like the scarlet-orange *R.* 'Koster's Brilliant Red' and golden *R.* 'Narcissiflorum'. Those I mention are popular as garden shrubs but I would urge you to visit woodland gardens or study specialist catalogues to see many others. Combining rhododendrons and azaleas requires care to avoid a clash of warm tones with cold ones like warm pink *R.* 'Hinomayo' and magenta *R.* 'Hatsugiri', so aim to keep them apart in different areas of the garden. But some colours, such as fresh light yellows, can be used as a buffer between them; try the tall primrose-yellow azalea *R. lutescens*, or slightly smaller *R.* 'Queen Elizabeth II', with pale lemon-yellow flowers. The dark purples also work well with both tones.

Beneath these magnificent shrubs, cover the ground with acid-loving associates like grey-jade leaved *Pachysandra terminalis* and its variegated form, colourful trilliums and white-flowered *Cardamine trifoliata*. Or include swathes of fragrant English bluebells in spring and, later, the lovely *Lilium martagon* in rose-purple or white forms.

Add bulk with shrubby evergreens like skimmias, pieris and gaultheria. But in damper soils, lighten the solidity of the evergreen mass with herbaceous companions such as luscious white-flowered *Smilacena racemosa* or the cool tones of feathery astilbes, that offer a great range of colours as well as heights. Consider rose-pink *Astilbe* 'Cattleya', at 1m (3ft) tall, or the deep red *A.* 'Fanal' at half the height. In damp conditions, primulas are invaluable, for example the purple-pinks of the exquisite *Primula pulverulenta* Bartley hybrids, as well as the fresh, light yellow of giant cowslips (*Primula florindae*).

summer colour

By summer the leaf canopy is at its most dense, so seek out the partially shaded areas for plants like foxgloves, which may be purple, pink or white. *Digitalis purpurea* f. *albiflora* is 1.2m (4ft) tall and lights up areas of partial shade particularly well. Add sparkle with *Aconitum* 'Ivorine' with its light-giving, creamy flower spikes, or the taller, dark blue form *A.* 'Spark's Variety'. Damp-loving shade plants like astilbes mix well with hostas that offer leaf as well as flower colour. From the tall, massed glaucous *Hosta* 'Big Daddy' to the tiny, dark green *H. venusta*, the range encompasses smooth leaves, deeply ribbed leaves, frilled, flat and slim ones. The leaf colours may be buttercup-yellow as in *H. fortunei* var. *albopicta* f. *aurea*, more acid like *H.* 'Zounds' or blue as in *H. sieboldiana* and the smaller, pretty *H.* 'Halcyon'. Variegated leaves have much charm in shade so look for the classic *H.* 'Frances Williams' or tiny *H.* 'Ginko Craig'.

A SMALL WOODLAND AREA IN SPRING

The effect of a spring woodland can be reproduced in a smallish garden by planting three Swedish birches (*Betula pendula* 'Dalecarlica') to create dappled shade beneath them. In the deeper shade below the trees, plants include the reedy leaves of *Luzula sylvatica* 'Variegata', evergreen *Iris foetidissima* 'Citrina' with modest yellow flowers, and ferns (*Polystichum setiferum* Acutilobum Group). Green-flowered *Helleborus foetidus* and, later on, foxgloves and martagon lilies will do well. Early in the year the large variegated leaves of blue-flowered *Brunnera macrophylla* 'Hadspen Cream' cover the ground and, to the front, other large leaves will unfold later, such as those of *Hosta* 'Ground Master' whose undulating green leaves have cream margins. In the centre is a run of wood spurge (*Euphorbia amygdaloides* 'Rubra') with maroon stems, dark green leaves and lime-yellow bracts. Further into the light, massed primroses appear beside lilac-coloured *Corydalis flexuosa* 'China Blue' opposite a stretch of blue-and-white *Anemone blanda*, all of which look wonderful in spring. These are closely followed by a drift of warm yellow-flowered, grassy-leaved *Hemerocallis dumortieri* at the edge of the shaded area.

opposite above: **In spring Spanish bluebells (*Hyacinthoides hispanica*) are perfect associates for white tulips at the edge of woodland.**

opposite below: **The flaming changes of autumn are superb in lightly shaded woodland, where glorious acers, parrotia and dogwoods increase the colour temperature. But the colours of fall are never better than those displayed by the Japanese maples (*Acer palmatum*).**

Planting styles for hot, dry, brightly lit gardens derive their inspiration from the kind of vegetation that thrives in the wild in Mediterranean-type climates. This term applies to areas with long, hot, dry summers where the winters are mild and have some rain, although the amount varies from country to country. These countries include the Cape in South Africa, some coastal parts of California, central Chile and southern parts of Australia, as well as the rim of the Mediterranean itself. The plants are those that revel in summer heat and can conserve water or manage on very little. A good proportion of them are evergreen, to absorb the wetness of winter and store it against summer's deprivation. Their foliage may be thick and glossily green, like that of the Chinese shrub *Pittosporum tobira*, or the fattened leaves of succulents like the many crassulas. Many shrubs have silvery foliage because of the fine hairs that cover the leaves, giving them a protective coating which reflects heat and drying sunlight. Such foliage prevents scorching as it shields the life-giving green chlorophyll inside the leaf. Other leaves may be fine and slim, like forms of indigenous *Rosmarinus officinalis*, or needle-like, such as those of the umbrella pine (*Pinus pinea*), making the foliage colour less distinct and the effect softer.

right: **A mass of lavenders beside and beneath shapely olive trees in Provence capture the essence of the Mediterranean planting style.**

bright light

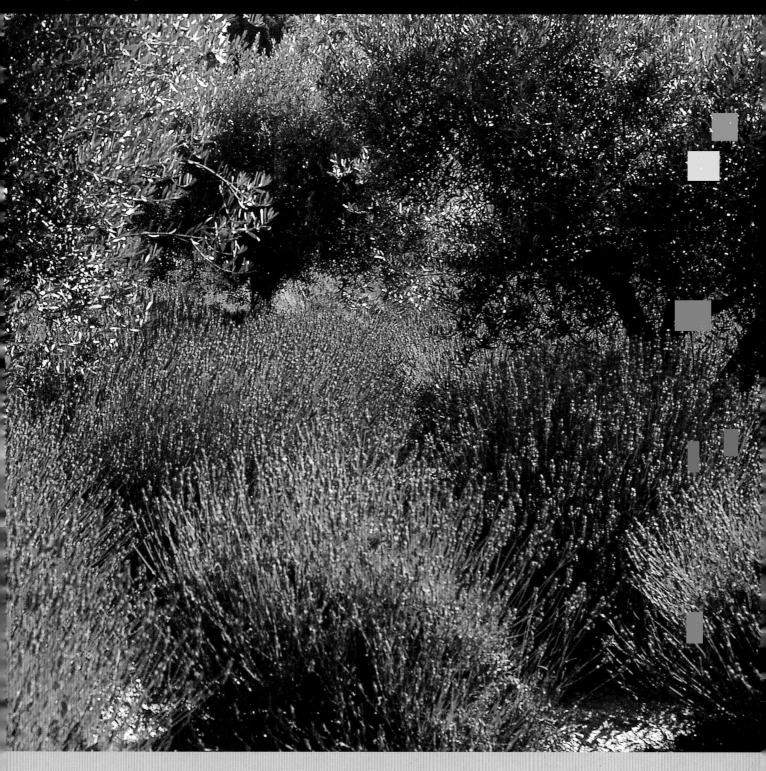

silver-grey foliage

Flowers come and go but leaves are there for much of the summer and sometimes longer. There are many silver-leaved plants to be relished in a hot, sunny climate, where they are as refreshing as an iced drink. As a linking element in the garden, silver foliage is invaluable (see Balance, page 86) for uniting the scheme.

Artemisias provide much of the 'ever-silver' backcloth in Mediterranean-climate gardens. They take many forms and textures – some are extremely silvery, like the filigree leaves of the low mound-forming *Artemisia alba* 'Canescens', whereas others may be greyer, like *A. lactiflora*, a tall, more clumpy plant. I like the little *A. schmidtiana* 'Nana', a silvery carpet, and the reliable *A.* 'Powis Castle', whose tall, feathery silver foliage soothes the herbaceous melée.

The lightness of silver foliage makes an ideal contrast with darker values, especially the deep red foliage shrubs, like forms of cotinus or berberis, that can look a bit morose. But the silvery contrast enriches such colours and reveals their subtle depths. For example, the flashing silver foliage of *Elaeagnus angustifolia* consorts well with the smaller *Cotinus coggygria* 'Royal Purple' and *Buddleja fallowiana* would fit in superbly, having slim grey foliage and long lavender-blue flower panicles in late summer. On a smaller scale, the dark plum *Weigela florida* 'Foliis Purpureis' is a rather nondescript small shrub once its light pink flowers have gone, but silver-white *Artemisia ludoviciana* var. *latiloba*, artfully placed, enhances both stages.

Other silver-leaved plants fit into the flower border well and many have flowers too, like old-fashioned garden pinks. The low-spreading, hardy *Anthemis punctata* subsp. *cupaniana* has white daisy flowers in early summer among its finely cut silver-grey foliage. If trimmed when they are finished, the plant often flowers again later. Taller *Achillea* 'Moonshine' has feathery-fine silver foliage with light yellow flowers. Smaller hebes, particularly *Hebe pinguifolia* 'Pagei' at only 30cm (12in) high, make permanent pewter-grey ground cover. The miniature *Tanacetum densum* subsp. *amani* is a woody, ever-silver plant for edging borders or growing in gravel. Its wide-spreading, silver-white woolly foliage resembles tiny ferns and is only 15cm (6in) high until the flat corymbs of yellow daisy flowers appear.

MEDITERRANEAN GRAVEL PLANTING

Repetition of plants and colours helps to link the three plant groups together. Foliage is often narrow, fleshy or silvered, all characteristics that conserve water. The bed to the left is dominated by tall *Coronilla valentina* subsp. *glauca*, an evergreen shrub with bluish foliage and yellow pea flowers. To its right is a mass of arching, blue grassy *Helictotrichon sempervirens*, with the grey foliage of *Arctotis acaulis*; the latter also has brilliant daisy flowers in orange, gold and mahogany. Two rock roses, *Helianthemum* 'Red Orient' and *H.* 'Double Yellow', echo these colours and merge with the grey woolly carpeting *Thymus lanuginosus*. Some *Lilium* 'Royal Gold' appear in summer, seen through the wispy grass *Stipa tenuissima*, while dark purple *Sedum maximum* 'Atropurpureum' is balanced by purple alliums elsewhere. These colours are repeated on the right, where a creeping yellow *Hypericum balearicum* grows by *Rosmarinus officinalis* 'Prostratus' and silver-leaved *Convolvulus cneorum*. The variegated yucca dominates, with another purple sedum to its right, soft lavender-blue *Nepeta sibirica* behind and more stipas in front. Three compact hebes, *Hebe ochracea* 'James Stirling', edge the bed. Many plants, such as the lilies, are replicated in the lower bed, where the distinguishing shrub is the large, evergreen *Cistus ladanifer*, with crimson-blotched white flowers.

Two much-used low evergreen grey shrubs – lavender and cotton lavender (*Santolina chamaecyparissus*) – are easily managed in clipped form, making them ideal as dwarf hedges. Their neutral silver-grey is a perfect foil for gently coloured herbs, roses of all colours and pastel summer bedding. But their flowers need taking into account. Those of the santolina are bright mustard-yellow, which can be difficult to relate to other plants, so many gardeners cut them off. But most lavender flowers are cool-toned lilac, mauve, pink or purple, making a soft complement to many colour schemes.

above: **Massed silver-white** ***Eryngium maritimum*,** **revelling in the heat, is** **luminous in front of the** **silver willows and** **gunnera in the damper** **soil behind.**

right: **A fine specimen of** ***Kniphofia* 'Percy's Pride'.**

silvers and blues

Grey-silver foliage sometimes has an overall blue tone and this too is a great foil in the multi-coloured herbaceous bed. Probably the best examples are the eryngiums, prickly leaved perennials with thistle-like flowers, which can be used to establish a cool tone to a planting scheme. *Eryngium* x *oliverianum* is provocative among mixed planting, having branching stems with silver-blue spiky bracts around a dome of similarly coloured flowers. Set among a mass of frost-hardy, softly sensual penstemons, the spiny eryngium appears positively barbed, but such subtly flattering association intensifies the colours. Consider with it *Penstemon* 'Alice Hindley', with rich purple-blue-and-pink flowers, or the lower-growing, paler, luminous *P.* 'Stapleford Gem'.

Alternatively, the eryngium could be used in a more emphatic way, for bold contrast, if it were grown with gold *Rudbeckia fulgida* var. *sullivantii* 'Goldsturm' and a run of carmine *Kniphofia* 'Timothy', soothed by a drift of pink-brown sedge (*Carex petrei*). If the blue-leaved grassy *Helictotrichon sempervirens* were included as well, the two blues would unite to produce an almost fluorescent effect among the other colours.

left: **Sharing a hot, gravelly site are the silvery blades of *Astelia nervosa* with grey-leaved, purple-flowered erysimums, scented geraniums and dwarf hebes, all of which blend with the fleshy jade-green echeverias in flower. Bold, black *Aeonium* 'Zwartkop' is a strong, assertive colour contrast.**

opposite: **Self-sown golden *Eschscholzia californica* mixes well with hot-coloured yellow-and-orange gazanias and creamy osteospermums, all enjoying their stony, sun-filled site. These colours have a jewel brilliance in strong sunlight.**

trees to give shade

When the light is unforgivingly strong, the effect on a garden is to reduce the three-dimensional qualities of the space and flatten its depth, so that shadows become razor-sharp and black. Trees are therefore important to restore the sense of space and provide relief from blazing sun in open sites. The choice of tree will depend on the size of the garden but all flower colours will look better if grown with some trees and evergreen shrubs, to provide contrast.

For a dense canopy in a large garden, the black mulberry (*Morus nigra*), with its dark red-purple fruits, is a tall, wide-spreading tree whose substantial green foliage casts deep shade and adds drama to an overheated garden. It comes from warm places but, liking cool winters, it is hardy. Wind is an enemy, however, and the tree does best on alkaline soils. The fig (*Ficus carica* 'Brown Turkey'), at 3m (10ft), has a wide canopy of beautiful large, jade-green lobed leaves that make it worth growing for ornamental reasons, although in cool areas it serves best against a warm wall. The evergreen olive (*Olea europaea*) is now surviving further north than used to be expected, so is worth considering for its attractive silvery grey-green lanceolate foliage. It is also compact, at about 10m (33ft) high and wide, and so is eminently suitable for the smaller garden. Neither the fig nor the olive likes frost so position is important.

For less substantial foliage and more dappled shade, consider the half-hardy evergreen silver wattle (*Acacia dealbata*), which is covered with mimosa-yellow flowers in late winter to spring among its floating glaucous-silver leaves. This tree is 15–30m (50–100ft) high but eye-catching height is an important linking part of the design. *Albizia julibrissin*, the silk tree, is much smaller at 6m (20ft).

Casting light shade, with fine, feathery leaves, it has silky yellowish or apricot terminal flowers. For really water-conserving foliage, the small wispy *Tamarix tetandra* is hardy and will be covered in fluffy light pink flowers by late summer, but it casts little shade.

Many Mediterranean shrubs will add a deep green background colour, for example the hardy honey spurge (*Euphorbia mellifera*), with narrow leaves that terminate in bronze cymes. Another is the half-hardy Japanese mock orange, evergreen *Pittosporum tobira*, with fragrant cream flowers in summer, that will ultimately be a tree 10m (33ft) high. Both greens would provide a good foil for the golden-orange spears of *Kniphofia* 'Bees' Sunset' complemented by the deep blue globes of *Echinops bannaticus* 'Taplow Blue' through summer. For a really small garden, *Choisya* 'Aztec Pearl' would be ideal, its pinkish white, highly scented flowers set off well against its narrow, glossy dark green leaves. A perfect companion would be *Convolvulus cneorum*, because of its paper-white flowers and silky-smooth, shimmering silver-grey leaves. To add sparkle, *Diascia rigescens* carries rose-pink flower spikes through the summer.

colour associations

With such evergreens as background and silver-foliaged plants also fitted in, you may like to try the bold colour of African kniphofias, South African gazanias, Peruvian alstroemerias and California poppies (*Eschscholzia*). These plants will give a full range of yellow, orange, scarlet and pink colours, delivering the panache of a carnival. For height, you could add *Abutilon* x *hybridum* 'Cloth of Gold' with yolk-yellow flowers. It is fast growing and may be pruned as a small tree to give a little dappled shade.

For a bright summer mood you might include half-hardy annuals like South African *Arctotis* x *hybrida* as a source of rich daisy flowers that carpet the ground with superb red, orange, bronze and deep pink colouring set off by jade-green rosette foliage. Choose named varieties like 'Mahogany', 'Tangerine', 'Red Magic', 'Apricot' and 'Terracotta'. They all prefer dry, gravelly soil. With such a blaze of colour, you could include darker-coloured permanent herbaceous plants like the glaucous-leaved red-purple *Sedum telephium* subsp. *maximum* 'Atropurpureum', a fleshy-leaved plant that revels in hot, dry conditions, and, for more contrast, the dark spode-blue flowers of greyish-leaved catmint (*Nepeta sibirica* 'Souvenir d'André Chaudron').

A totally different approach would be to choose blues as the foundation of a Mediterranean-climate scheme. The frost-tender *Echium candicans*, with flower spires up to 2.5m (8ft) tall of an intensely blue-purple, could set the pace – but these are big plants. I always think of statice (*Limonium latifolium* 'Blue Cloud') as the poor man's echium, with smaller lilac-blue masses of flower spikes in late summer, but the colour and dry, tactile texture seem similar. The silver-blue forms of both eryngiums and echinops would make good summer associates, particularly with grey and purple sages (varieties of *Salvia officinalis*) and silvery artemisias. The lush emerald foliage of agapanthus could introduce a fresher note: choose from the small blue *Agapanthus* 'Lilliput' to the tall violet-blue *A. caulescens*. As a dashing inclusion for late summer, magenta *Lychnis coronaria*, with its grey leaves, would be a wonderful clash. Or you may like to plant areas of tall 'see-through' fluorescent light purple *Verbena bonariensis*, another late flowerer that sways in the wind, having flowerheads at the end of the slim stalks, 2m (6ft) above ground.

Clumps of summer-flowering red valerian (*Centranthus ruber*) could also be included; its blue-toned crimson flowers and fleshy grey-green leaves would fit in nicely with the subtle scheme. There is a white form too, and this would enliven the mass. Or you might try evergreen reedy *Libertia grandiflora*, a perennial for early summer, followed by woolly-white *Ballota acetabulosa* through the season, with the later white umbels of *Agapanthus* 'Albus' to follow.

cooling gravel

In a Mediterranean climate, the ground is bone dry in summer and often stony. The gardener can interpret this as a gravel garden. A 5cm (2in) layer of washed gravel will cool roots, cut down evaporation and provide frost protection for Mediterranean-climate plants. There are many types of gravel, so choose a colour that blends with the local area and lay sheets of a weed-impermeable geotextile beneath the gravel to keep out weeds before making planting holes for your chosen plants. The gravel should be seen to flow over the whole area so that paths are distinguished only because there will be no plants growing there.

Introduce more flower colour here with the magenta-purple flowers of *Lavandula stoechas*, perhaps associated with lemon-yellow achilleas and a few groups of the small ivory *Kniphofia* 'Little Maid'. Spreading mats of grey-leaved light yellow *Stachys byzantina* 'Primrose Heron' would associate well with *Helianthemum* 'Wisley Primrose' and pink-flowered, grey-leaved *Thymus doerfleri* 'Bressingham', perhaps with gritty-looking silver-grey *Raoulia australis* and bronze-blue *Acaena* 'Blue Haze'. You could include *Verbena* 'La France' to relate to the lavender because of its continuous summer display of violet-blue flowers. And try to echo the woolly stachys foliage nearby with *Phlomis tuberosa* 'Amazone', whose whorls of dusky-pink flowers are repeated along the stem, and *Nepeta tuberosa*, another felted plant with blue- and wine-coloured flower spires. For the contrast of its sharp, sword-shaped silver leaves, I would include *Celmisia semicordata* which also has white daisy flowers.

Travel has widened our expectations so that we often wish to include 'exotic' plants even in temperate-climate gardens. Possible climate changes mean that many such plants are now proving hardy enough to be risked in certain situations, providing a wonderful opening for gardeners. What do we mean by exotic? If the term simply means from a foreign place, this applies to many garden plants. After all, our herbaceous beds contain plants from every continent – even roses and rhododendrons have travelled across the world. In horticultural terms, exotic has come to suggest plants of a sub-tropical origin, most of which are tender to some degree. But as it also conjures up unusual and dramatic shapes, we can include in these schemes hardy plants that are not sub-tropical but look as if they could be.

above: **Colourful foliage is the theme of this sub-tropical grouping of plants. Frost-tender *Acaphylla wilkensiana*, known widely as copperleaf, can be seen with *Codiaeum* and purple fountain grass (*Pennisetum setaceum* 'Purpureum') against a superb backdrop of mountains in Mauritius.**

right: **Exotic plants native to their Tucson landscape thrive in the blazing heat of Arizona. Jade-coloured prickly pears (*Opuntia*) and agaves look fluorescent against the rocky landscape. Pink colouring comes from *Lantana montevidensis*.**

exotic style

the exotic style

This style of planting is not for the faint-hearted: it is bold, dramatic and exciting. Foliage is important to set the scene and most of it is large, so you do need space. Much will be green but this covers the exciting shapes of fan palms, hardy bananas, yuccas and cordylines. If in doubt about your situation, the sharp green Mediterranean *Chamaerops humilis* is the hardiest fan palm but there is a form, *C. humilis* var. *cerifera*, from North Africa, which has waxy foliage of steely blue, similar to that of the half-hardy Mexican blue palm (*Brahea armata*). These plants may reach 2.5–3m (8–10ft) high. *Musa basjoo* is a hardy banana with massive paddle-shaped leaves that will need to be out of the wind, or they will shred. So provide warm shelter and rich, moist soil with regular watering and feeding through summer. Wrap it up warmly in winter.

Yuccas are the temperate man's agave: the leaves of these hardy stalwarts are rigid and dangerously sharp and the flowers tower above them, usually as massed creamy bells. There is a golden-striped form, *Yucca filamentosa* 'Bright Edge', whose panicles may be over 2m (6ft) tall. Never plant yuccas where children play. A shiver of bamboos would make a good companion, like gold *Phyllostachys aurea* or black *P. nigra*, both reaching to 5m (15ft).

The greenness of these great leaves creates a unity in the garden, so that green light filters through to ground level, affecting the appearance of all colours beneath. This 'jungle' effect emulates the dark green depths of the rainforest, with its flowers mostly high overhead. But in the garden we want colour at eye level and at ground level, so spaces should be provided within the encircling low-lit areas, which are open to the sun. And here we can plant flowers and foliage with brilliant colour.

Colour and drama may be supplied by purple lance-leaved cabbage palms (*Cordyline australis* 'Atropurpureum' or 'Torbay Red'), both of which grow 3–10m (10–33ft) high. Other colourful large

providing the right conditions

In order to include truly sub-tropical plants, the site must be naturally warm and you will have to manage it to avoid all exposure to wind and frost. Or you can hedge the site about to create an artificially protected microclimate. In town gardens, use vine-clad trellis on a warm boundary wall, rather than planting overhanging trees that drip cold water all through winter. In areas where the climate is unreliable, you will have to wrap plants with horticultural fleece for winter or grow them in large containers, preferably on castors, so that they can be taken into a conservatory or garden room where central heating may save them. Always make sure that these plants never stand in cold, wet soil – snow may provide a warm blanket but when it thaws there will be a problem, and a late-spring frost causes even more damage. Provide very rich, moist soil and keep it up to standard by adding more nutrients every year. If you have long, dry summers or intend to plant in the rainshadow of a wall, consider installing an automatic watering system.

above left: **In a temperate garden, the massive purple columnar cymes of woody, frost-tender** *Echium wildpretii* **dominate even the fan palm (***Trachycarpus fortunei***) and a variegated phormium (***Phormium cookianum* **subsp.** *hookeri* **'Cream Delight').**

left: **Exotic-looking but not tender, the dark red furry bottlebrush (***Callistemon***) contrasts with yellow** *Spartium junceum*.

leaves will help create the exciting, sometimes overpowering, atmosphere of the exotic garden style. *Beschorneria yuccoides*, a yucca-like plant, has sharp, fleshy lance-like grey leaves and produces tall panicles of chocolate-crimson bracts with greenish-cream flowers. This plant will need covering for winter and must have well-drained soil. Watsonias are cormous perennials with sword-shaped leaves that can be 40cm–1m (16in–3ft) tall, with the bonus of superb tall flower spires. *Watsonia* 'Tresco Hybrid' has tubular flowers of orange, pink and scarlet. Being only half-hardy, watsonias must be well covered against cold and wet in winter.

As a contrast, try planting the South African honey bush (*Melianthus major*), which is frost-hardy to frost-tender. Its glaucous to silvery foliage is soft and lush and the large leaves are prettily toothed; spiked racemes of deep red flowers enhance the foliage in a warm summer.

brilliant colour

The exotic style is all about bold, vivid colour and, given sunlight, there are many flowers that can provide it. The ginger lily (*Hedychium gardnerianum*) is a half-hardy plant from north India, growing to 2.2m (7ft). It has superb, large lance-shaped leaves from which emerges a cylinder of yellow flower trumpets with long crimson stamens. Grown in a group with very light shade and moist soil, it is spectacular. You could echo the colour elsewhere with Mexican *Agastache cusickii* 'Firebird', a bushy hardy perennial with aromatic green foliage and copper-coloured flower spikes 30cm (12in) high in mid- to late summer. For a dramatic colour clash, consider the 'marvel of Peru', the frost tender 60cm (2ft) tall *Mirabilis jalapa* with its red, magenta, pink, white or yellow flowers, often on the same plant. This flowers from early to late summer, provided that it has protection and is never drowned.

AN EXOTIC LOOK FOR A SMALL GARDEN

Even small garden spaces in temperate countries can emulate the exotic look. Here, black bamboo (*Phyllostachys nigra*) oversees dramatic foliage shapes and strong colour. On the left, the hardy fan palm, *Chamaerops humilis* var. *cerifera*, has large bluish leaves; to its right, standing at the back, is another boldly foliaged plant, *Cordyline australis* 'Purple Tower', displaying massed sword-shaped leaves flushed red-purple over green. Needing to be dominant in such company, the brilliant flame-coloured *Kniphofia* 'Royal Standard' has scarlet-topped columnar flowers; their narrow greyed leaves link with the fan palm. Between these groups of high-impact plants is a run of apricot-yellow *Crocosmia* 'Solfatare', with bronzed foliage echoing the dark brown leaves of *Dahlia* 'Bishop of Llandaff', whose large vermilion flowers have a yellow eye. Footing the whole ensemble is *Ophiopogon planiscapus* 'Nigrescens' whose black grassy foliage links with the black bamboo canes.

For situations with hot summers, such bold clashes may be furthered by *Dahlia merkii*, a tuberous-rooted branching perennial from Mexico that has proved itself in warm districts, where it blooms continuously throughout summer. The small flowers are lilac with a central maroon cone that has yellow stamens and it can grow up to 2m (6ft). I would also consider planting the large, half-hardy *Geranium maderense*, which offers a similar magenta colour in its generous flower sprays that last throughout summer, surrounded by a collar of lush foliage. This fine geranium stands out whatever the company. Both plants must have good drainage and cover during cold, wet winters.

For dramatic intervals, you could include some dark colour contrast with temporary summer planting. The tall *Canna iridiflora* 'King Humbert' has purple-black paddle-shaped leaves 1m (3ft) long and bright red orchid-like flowers. The castor-oil plant (*Ricinus communis* 'Impala') has dark brown-black palmate leaves up to 45cm (18in) long and greenish-yellow flower spikes that reach 1.8m (6ft) in height. To add clashing scintillation, orange tiger lilies (*Tigridia*) or brightly coloured daylilies like *Hemerocallis* 'Gold Pride' or *H.* 'Stafford' could be companions.

exotics in an urban situation

The enclosed urban courtyard in which temperatures are a few degrees warmer than normal will have boundary walls, an asset for foundation planting. You can exploit the range of tender climbers with brilliantly coloured flowers that need protection. Deciduous *Campsis grandiflora* is a fully- to frost-hardy Chinese plant with orange-scarlet panicles of wide-mouthed tubular flowers at their best in late summer. A reliable variety is *Campsis* x *tagliabuana* 'Madame Galen' with large salmon-red flowers and dark leaves, which yellow in autumn. Growing up to 10m (33ft), it twines and is not self-clinging; bear in mind that this plant is late in leaf and rather slow to flower.

Two evergreen Chilean climbers offer vibrant colour: the Chilean bellflower (*Lapageria rosea*) is a woody climber with rich red or shell-pink tubular flowers that holds on by twining around wires or trellis. The Chilean glory flower (*Eccremocarpus scaber*) also has red flowers and rambles, so it needs training. Being frost-hardy to frost-tender, both need protection in a warm, sheltered spot in sun or light shade.

A good companion for such climbers would be massed *Asclepias tuberosa*, a frost-tender tuberous perennial whose unusual lance-like leaves spiral around the 1m (3ft) high stem and terminal umbels of orange-red or yellow flowers appear from mid- to late summer. For late-season powerful colour, look at the semi-evergreen orange-flowered *Leonotis leonurus*, an erect shrub of the same height.

With their exciting hot colours, many tuberous plants could be an asset for the urban site, like early-summer *Sparaxis tricolor*, a cormous plant from South Africa with grass-like foliage and bright orange, red or purple flowers. Many gladiolus hybrids would be perfect for providing additional brilliant colour. *Gladiolus* Grandiflorus Group flowers from early to late summer; plant in groups of odd numbers but do not mix within the group because a single colour will have more impact en masse. Hybrid gladioli can be very tall (up to 1.7m/5ft 6in) like the coffee-coloured *Gladiolus* 'Mileesh', cerise *G.* 'Cherry Pie', blood-red *G.* 'Anitra', mid-blue *G.* 'Blue Delight' and blue *G.* 'Cote d'Azur'. There are some smaller varieties, like golden *G.* 'Georgette', at 1.2m (4ft), or, even lower, an unusual salmon-pink-with-lemon, *G.* 'Little Darling'. *G.* 'Firestorm', smaller again at 1m (3ft), has ruffled vivid scarlet flowers flecked with gold, neatly spaced up the stem.

left above: **Glowing *Kniphofia rooperi* duplicates the explosive colour relationship between orange *Canna* 'Striata' and the scarlet cactus dahlia, with a background of golden-yellow helianthus.**

left: **Ever dramatic, the hardy *Crocosmia* 'Lucifer' is displayed effectively in front of a red-leaved canna.**

right: **A grassy path invites you to walk through exotic sub-tropical borders vying with one another for brilliant colour. The plants include begonias, impatiens, alocasia, dracaenas and epiphytic** *Platycerium bifurcatum,* **drawing its strength from the tree.**

exotic leaves for shade

Exotic may suggest a hot, sun-filled site but the sub-tropical forests have dense leafy canopies. So, for dramatic effect, part of your garden can emulate this, firstly by making the most of existing shade and secondly by choosing thickly canopied tall plants like the loquat (*Eriobotrya japonica*), a small tree 8m by 8m (25ft by 25ft), or perhaps a magnolia like evergreen *Magnolia grandiflora* 'Goliath', at 6–8m (20–25ft) tall, which also has very large ivory flowers. Such trees will create areas with low greenish light under which you can grow lush ferns like the European chain fern (*Woodwardia radicans*) with thick, lance-shaped but finely toothed dark green fronds, or the Japanese holly fern (*Cyrtomium falcatum*), which is fully- to frost-hardy and best planted in a protected semi-shaded area, for more dark green lush foliage.

As long as the soil is kept moist, arum lilies (*Zantedeschia aethiopica* 'Crowborough') will do well in light shade; their large leaves are joined by tall ivory-white spathes. Look also for the glaucous form, 'Green Goddess'. You could include some bulbous plants, like tall *Leucojum aestivum* 'Gravetye Giant' for its white flowers in spring, and lilies that enjoy light shade, such as the spotted gold *Lilium* 'Citronella', which has elegantly reflexed petals. *Clivia miniata*, a South African frost-tender evergreen that grows in woodland, can also walk on the shady side. It has strap-like leaves and large umbels of tubular yellow, red or orange flowers. In fertile, humus-rich soil, it will grow to 45cm (18in). For the winter garden, green-flowering *Helleborus foetidus* would look suitably exotic.

imitation exotics

Among the non sub-tropical plants that have an 'exotic' shape are hardy bulbous plants with sculpted flowers such as lilies and these could be planted in small groups. Where they have well-drained soil, they may last for several years. *Lilium* 'African Queen' looks exotic because of its distinctive 1.5m (5ft) high spires of apricot-orange trumpet flowers. Similar in shape, deep yellow *L.* 'Golden Splendour' can grow up to 2m (6ft) tall; its colour could be balanced by the smaller *L.* 'Monte Negro', with deep maroon-red open flowers. Crimson *L.* 'Stargazer' has white-edged petals and is highly scented. 'Fake' exotic plants like these fit in well with the true exotics.

For a blast of colour, try massed Peruvian lilies (*Alstroemeria* Ligtu hybrids), tuberous hardy perennials crammed with small, highly coloured lily-like flowers in orange, soft apricot, amber-yellow, old gold, ruby, dusty pink and cinnamon, each marked with deep red, purple or brown streaks along the inner petals. Weave them among other herbaceous perennials to stretch the imagination towards 'exotic'. Consider red hot pokers such as *Kniphofia* 'Prince Igor', a tall column of rich orange-scarlet in late summer, or the slightly smaller red-and-yellow *K.* 'Atlanta' for early summer, followed in midsummer by *K.* 'Shining Sceptre', a yellow flushed orange. Include the smaller *Gazania* Chansonette Series for more electric colour. Crocosmias, with their sword-shaped leaves, make exotic-looking companions, with brilliantly coloured flowers to match, like the popular fiery-red *C.* 'Lucifer', over 1m (3ft) tall, and smaller *C.* 'Solfatare', with apricot-yellow flowers and bronze leaves.

plant lists

plant lists by colour

I refer to a great number of plants in this book. Many are familiar, some have become available in recent years, while others are real newcomers, hybrids from the growers. The *RHS Plant Finder* is an excellent source guide for the UK and *PPP Index* will assist those in other countries to find the plants. Both books are revised annually.

Of course readers will have favourites of their own and many will want to experiment. For the planting schemes suggested throughout the book, substitution is always possible and the lists that follow suggest alternatives within a particular colour category. Height and spread are of course relevant and are given throughout (except for climbers), in addition to any special conditions required, such as acid soil or damp conditions.

a note on plant hardiness

The terms used throughout the book wherever relevant to describe a plant's hardiness are defined as follows:

Hardy plants can withstand temperatures down to -15°C (5°F)

Frost-hardy plants can withstand temperatures down to -5°C (23°F)

Half-hardy plants can withstand temperatures down to 0°C (32°F)

Frost-tender plants may be damaged by temperatures below 5°C (41°F)

reds
intense reds (scarlet, blood red)

PERENNIALS

Astilbe 'Fanal'
  45cm by 40cm (18in by 16in) (damp soil)
Crocosmia 'Lucifer'
  1.2m by 8cm (4ft by 3in)
Geum 'Mrs J. Bradshaw'
  60cm by 60cm (2ft by 24ft)
Hemerocallis 'Christmas Is'
  80cm by 1m (32in by 3ft)
Hemerocallis 'Stafford'
  70cm by 1m (28in by 3ft)
Heuchera 'Red Spangles'
  50cm by 25cm (20in by 10in)
Kniphofia 'Prince Igor'
  1.6m by 90cm (5ft 6in by 3ft)
Lychnis x *arkwrightii* 'Vesuvius'
  45cm by 30cm (18in by 1ft)
Lychnis chalcedonica
  1.2m by 30cm (4ft by 1ft)
Monarda 'Cambridge Scarlet'
  90cm by 45cm (3ft by 18in)
Papaver orientale 'Beauty of Livermere'
  1.2m by 90cm (4ft by 3ft)
Papaver orientale 'Turkenlouis'
  90cm by 90cm (3ft by 3ft)
Potentilla 'Etna'
  45cm by 60cm (18in by 2ft)
Potentilla 'Flamenco'
  45cm by 60cm (18in by 2ft)
Potentilla 'Volcan'
  60cm by 60cm (2ft by 2ft)
Schizostylis coccinea 'Major'
  60cm by 30cm (2ft by 1ft)

SHRUBS

Rhododendron 'Koster's Brilliant Red'
  1.2m by 1.2m (4ft by 4ft) (acid soil)
Rosa Danse du Feu
  2.5m by 2.5m (8ft by 8ft)

CLIMBERS

Eccremocarpus scaber
Lapageria rosea

BULBS

Dahlia 'Alva's Doris'
  1.2m by 60cm (4ft by 2ft)
Dahlia 'Bishop of Llandaff'
  1.1m by 45cm (3ft 6in by 18in)
Gladiolus 'Anitra'
  1.7m by 15cm (5ft 6in by 6in)
Tulipa 'Couleur Cardinal'
  35cm (14in)

cool reds (crimson, cerise, magenta)

PERENNIALS

Achillea millefolium 'Cerise Queen'
  60cm by 60cm (2ft by 2ft)
Centranthus ruber
  1m by 1m (3ft by 3ft)
Geranium psilostemon
  90cm by 60cm (3ft by 2ft)
Geranium x *riversleaianum* 'Russell Prichard'
  30cm by 1m (1ft by 3ft)
Hemerocallis 'Summer Wine'
  60cm by 70cm (2ft by 28in)
Iris 'Gypsy Jewels'
  90cm by 80cm (3ft by 2ft 6in)
Lychnis coronaria
  80cm by 45cm (32in by 18in)
  (silver foliage)
  Penstemon 'Garnet'
  75cm by 60cm (2ft 6in by 2ft)
Phlox paniculata 'Starfire'
  90cm by 60cm (3ft by 2ft)
Tanacetum coccineum 'Brenda'
  80cm by 45cm (32in by 18in)

SHRUBS

Lavatera 'Burgundy Wine'
  2m by 2m (6ft by 6ft)
Rhododendron 'Cynthia'
  6m by 6m (20ft by 20ft) (acid soil)

BULBS

Gladiolus 'Cherry Pie'
  1.7m by 15cm (5ft 6in by 6in)

pale reds (pink, rose, dusty pink)

PERENNIALS

Anemone x *hybrida* 'Margaret' (syn. 'Lady Gilmour')
  1.2m by 1.2m (4ft by 4ft)
Astilbe x *arendsii* 'Cattleya'
  90cm by 60cm (3ft by 2ft)
Diascia rigescens
  30cm by 50cm (12in by 20in)
Filipendula purpurea
  1.2m by 60cm (4ft by 2ft) (damp soil)
Linaria purpurea 'Canon Went'
  90cm by 30cm (3ft by 1ft)
Malva moschata
  90cm by 60cm (3ft by 2ft)
Monarda 'Beauty of Cobham'
  90cm by 45cm (3ft by 18in)
Papaver orientale 'Cedric's Pink'
  90cm by 90cm (3ft by 3ft)
Papaver orientale 'Patty's Plum'
  75cm by 60cm (2ft 6in by 2ft)
Phlox paniculata 'Bright Eyes'
  1.2m by 60cm (4ft by 2ft)
Phlomis tuberosa 'Amazone'
  1.5m by 75cm (5ft by 2ft 6in)
Sidalcea malviflora 'Loveliness'
  75cm by 45cm (2ft 6in by 18in)
Sedum 'Herbstfeude' (syn. 'Autumn Joy')
  60cm by 60cm (2ft by 2ft)

SHRUBS

Deutzia x *elegantissima* 'Rosealind'
  1.2m by 1.5m (4ft by 5ft)
Fuchsia 'Jack Shahan'
  45cm by 60cm (18in by 2ft)
Geranium cinereum 'Ballerina'
  15cm by 30cm (6in by 12in)
Rhododendron 'Hino-mayo'
  60cm by 60cm (2ft by 2ft) (acid soil)

BULBS

Dahlia 'Conway'
  90cm by 60cm (3ft by 2ft)

dark reds (chocolate, wine, maroon)

PERENNIALS

Astrantia major 'Hadspen Blood'
  60cm by 45cm (2ft by 18in)
Cirsium rivulare 'Atropurpureum'
  1.2m by 60cm (4ft by 2ft)
Cosmos atrosanguineus
  75cm by 45cm (2ft 6in by 18in)
Geranium phaeum 'Samobor'
  80cm by 45cm (32in by 18in)
Iris 'Red Lion'
  90cm by 70cm (3ft by 28in)
Knautia macedonica
  80cm by 45cm (32in by 18in)
Paeonia officinalis 'Rubra Plena'
  75cm by 75cm (2ft 6in by 2ft 6in)
Penstemon 'Burgundy'
  90cm by 45cm (3ft by 18in)
Phlox paniculata 'Dusterlohe'
  1.2m by 60cm (4ft by 2ft)

SHRUBS

Fuchsia 'Margaret'
  1.2m by 1.2m (4ft by 4ft)
Rhododendron 'Purple Splendour'
  3m by 3m (10ft by 10ft) (acid soil)
Rosa 'Charles de Mills'
  1.2m by 1.2m (4ft by 4ft)
Rosa William Shakespeare
  1.2m by 1.2m (4ft by 4ft)

CLIMBERS

C. 'Niobe'
Rosa 'Guinée'
Rosa Sympathie

BULBS

Alstroemeria 'Margaret'
  1.1m by 75cm (3ft 6in by 2ft 6in)
Allium sphaerocephalon
  90cm by 8cm (3ft by 3in)
Lilium 'Black Beauty'
  2m by 40cm (6ft by 16in)
Lilium 'Monte Negro'
  60cm (2ft)
Tulipa 'Burgundy'
  55cm (22in)
Tulipa 'Queen of Night'
  70cm (28in)

ANNUALS

Helianthemum 'Velvet Queen'
 2m by 1.2m (6ft by 4ft)
Helianthus 'Claret'
 2m by 45cm (6ft by 18in)

blues
intense blues (cobalt, sapphire, cornflower)

PERENNIALS

Delphinium 'Atlantis'
 1– 1.2m by 90cm (3–4ft by 3ft)
Delphinium 'Blue Nile'
 1.7m by 90cm (5ft 6in by 3ft)
Echinops ritro 'Veitch's Blue'
 90cm by 45cm (3ft by 18in)
Geranium 'Rozanne'
 50cm by 90cm (18in by 3ft)
Geranium wallichianum 'Buxton's Variety'
 30cm by 1.2m (1ft by 4ft)
Salvia guaranitica 'Blue Enigma'
 1.5m by 90cm (5ft by 3ft)
Salvia nemorosa 'Ostfriesland' (syn. 'East Friesland')
 60cm by 45cm (2ft by 18in)
Veronica austriaca subsp. *teucrium* 'Crater Lake Blue'
 25cm by 40cm (10in by 16in)

SHRUBS

Ceratostigma plumbaginoides
 45cm by 30cm (18in by 12in)
Hibiscus syriacus 'Blue Bird'
 3m by 2m (10ft by 6ft)
Hydrangea macrophylla 'Blue Wave'
 1.5m by 2.5m (5ft by 8ft)
Rosmarinus officinalis 'Benenden Blue'
 1.5m by 1.5m (5ft by 5ft)

CLIMBERS

Clematis 'Polish Spirit'
Solanum crispum 'Glasnevin'

BULBS

Agapanthus 'Lilliput'
 40cm by 40cm (16in by 16in)

Agapanthus Headbourne hybrids
 90cm by 60cm (3ft by 2ft)
Gladiolus 'Blue Delight'
 1.7m by 15cm (5ft 6in by 6in)

ANNUALS

Nigella damascena 'Miss Jekyll'
 45cm by 23cm (18in by 9in)

pale blues (sky-blue, powder-blue, lavender)

PERENNIALS

Campanula lactiflora 'Prichard's Variety'
 1m by 60cm (3ft by 2ft)
Campanula persicifolia 'Telham Beauty'
 90cm by 30cm (3ft by 1ft)
Delphinium 'Blue Bees'
 1m by 1.2m (3ft by 4ft)
Geranium pratense 'Mrs Kendall Clark'
 80cm by 60cm (32in by 2ft)
Iris 'Jane Phillips'
 85cm (34in)
Iris sibirica 'Flight of Butterflies'
 75cm (2ft 6in)
Limonium latifolium 'Blue Cloud'
 60cm by 45cm (2ft by 18in)
Scabiosa caucasica 'Clive Greaves'
 75cm by 60cm (2ft 6in by 2ft)
Scabiosa 'Butterfly Blue'
 40cm by 40cm (16in by16in)

SHRUBS

Ceanothus 'Cascade'
 4m by 4m (12ft by 12ft)
Ceanothus 'Gloire de Versailles'
 1.5m by 1.5m (5ft by 5ft)
Perovskia atriplicifolia 'Blue Spire'
 1.2m by 1m (4ft by 3ft)

ANNUALS

Linum grandiflorum 'Caeruleum'
 45cm by 15cm (18in by 6in)
Nigella damascena
 40cm by 23cm (16in by 9in)

dark blues (prussian, indigo, ink, navy)

PERENNIALS

Aconitum 'Spark's Variety'
 1.2m by 1.5m (4ft by 5ft)
Aconitum carmichaelii
 1.8m by 40cm (6ft by 16in)
Agapanthus campanulatus 'Isis'
 75cm by 30cm (2ft 6in by 12in)
Agapanthus inapertus
 80cm by 60cm (32in by 2ft)
Delphinium 'Blue Tit'
 1.7m by 90cm (5ft 6in by 3ft)
Geranium ibericum
 45cm by 60cm (18in by 2ft)
Iris 'Titan's Glory'
 60cm (2ft)
Lupinus 'Blueberry Pie'
 90cm by 75cm (3ft by 2ft 6in)
Nepeta 'Souvenir d'André Chaudron'
 45cm by 45cm (18in by 18in)
Salvia patens
 60cm by 45cm (2ft by 18in)
Salvia x *sylvestris* 'Mainacht'
 70cm by 45cm (28in by 18in)

SHRUBS

Caryopteris x *clandonensis* 'Heavenly Blue'
 1m by 1.5m (3ft by 5ft)
Ceanothus 'Concha'
 2.5–3m by 3m (8–10ft by 10ft)

CLIMBERS

Clematis 'The President'
Clematis x *durandii*

ANNUALS

Myosotis sylvatica 'Ultramarine'
 15cm by 20cm (6in by 8in)
Salvia farinacea 'Victoria'
 60cm by 30cm (2ft by 1ft)

yellows
intense yellows (gold, buttercup, mustard)

PERENNIALS

Achillea filipendula 'Gold Plate'
1.2m by 45cm (4ft by 18in)
Centaurea macrocephala
1.5m by 60cm (5ft by 2ft)
Coreopsis grandiflora 'Early Sunrise'
45cm by 45cm (18in by 18in)
Coreopsis grandiflora 'Mayfield Giant'
90cm by 45cm (3ft by 18in)
Crocosmia x *crocosmiiflora* 'Solfatare'
60cm by 8cm (2ft by 3in)
Geum 'Lady Stratheden'
60cm by 60cm (2ft by 2ft)
Helenium 'Goldrausch'
1.5m by 60cm (5ft by 2ft)
Hemerocallis 'Berlin Yellow'
90cm by 90cm (3ft by 3ft)
Hemerocallis 'Corky'
70cm by 40cm (28in by 16in)
Inula magnifica
1.8m by 1m (6ft by 3ft)
Rudbeckia 'Herbstonne'
2m by 90cm (6ft by 3ft)
Rudbeckia fulgida var. *sullivantii* 'Goldsturm'
60cm by 45cm (2ft by 18in)
Rudbeckia laciniata 'Goldquelle'
90cm by 45cm (3ft by 18in)
Solidago 'Crown of Rays'
60cm by 45cm (2ft by 18in)
Solidago 'Linner Gold'
90cm by 45cm (3ft by 18in)
Thermopsis montana
90cm by 60cm (3ft by 2ft)
Verbascum 'Cotswold Queen'
1.2m by 30cm (4ft by 1ft)

SHRUBS

Coronilla valentina
1.5m by 1.5m (5ft by 5ft)

CLIMBERS

Fremontodendron 'California Glory'
Rosa 'Gloire de Dijon'

BULBS

Dahlia 'Yellow Hammer'
60cm by 45cm (2ft by 18in) (brown foliage)
Hedychium gardnerianum
2.2m by 90cm (7ft by 3ft) (tender)
Tulipa 'West Point'
50cm (20in)
Lilium 'Connecticut King'
1m by 40cm (3ft by 16in)
Lilium 'Golden Splendour'
2m by 40cm (6ft by 16in)

pale yellows (lemon, primrose, cream)

PERENNIALS

Achillea 'Taygetea'
60cm by 45cm (2ft by 18in)
Achillea x *lewisii* 'King Edward'
12cm by 23cm (5in by 9in)
Aconitum 'Ivorine'
90cm by 45cm (3ft by 18in)
Anthemis tinctoria 'E.C. Buxton'
45cm by 90cm (18in by 3ft)
Anthemis tinctoria 'Sauce Hollandaise'
60cm by 60cm (2ft by 2ft)
Argyranthemum frutescens 'Jamaica Primrose'
90cm by 90cm (3ft by 3ft)
Cephalaria gigantea
2.5m by 60cm (8ft by 2ft)
Coreopsis verticillata 'Moonbeam'
50cm by 45cm (20in by 18in)
Helianthus 'Lemon Queen'
1.7m by 1.2m (5ft 6in by 4ft)
Helichrysum 'Schwefellicht' (syn. 'Sulphur Light')
40cm by 30cm (16in by 12in) (grey foliage)
Hemerocallis 'Marion Vaughn'
85cm by 75cm (34in by 30in)
Kniphofia 'Little Maid'
60cm by 45cm (2ft by 18in)
Kniphofia 'Shining Sceptre'
1.2m by 60cm (4ft by 2ft)
Lupinus 'Chandelier'
90cm by 75cm (3ft by 2ft 6in)
Nepeta govaniana
90cm by 60cm (3ft by 2ft)
Phlomis russeliana
90cm by 75cm (3ft by 2ft 6in)

Sisyrinchium striatum
60cm by 60cm (2ft by 2ft)
Scabiosa columbaria var. *ochroleuca*
60cm by 40cm (2ft by 16in)
Thalictrum flavum subsp. *glaucum*
90cm by 60cm (3ft by 2ft)
Verbascum 'Gainsborough'
1.2m by 30cm (4ft by 1ft)

SHRUBS

Cytisus x *kewensis*
30cm by 1.5m (1ft by 5ft)
Helianthemum 'Wisley Primrose'
30cm by 45cm (1ft by 18in)
Lupinus arboreus
2m by 2m (6ft by 6ft)
Phygelius aequalis 'Yellow Trumpet'
90cm by 90cm (3ft by 3ft)
Potentilla fruticosa 'Primrose Beauty'
75cm by 1.2m (2ft 6in by 4ft)
Potentilla fruticosa 'Tilford Cream'
60cm by 1m (2ft by 3ft)
Rhododendron 'Chink'
60cm by 60cm (2ft by 2ft) (acid soil)
Santolina pinnata subsp. *neapolitana* 'Sulphurea'
75cm by 90cm (2ft 6in by 3ft) (grey foliage)
Santolina rosmarinifolia 'Primrose Gem'
60cm by 90cm (2ft by 3ft)
Santolina var. *corsica* 'Lemon Queen'
60cm by 60cm (2ft by 2ft)

purples
dark purples (deep violet, bishop's purple)

PERENNIALS

Campanula latifolia var. *macrantha*
90cm by 60cm (3ft by 2ft)
Delphinium 'Piccolo'
1–1.2m by 90cm (3–4ft by 3ft)
Geranium clarkei x *collinum* 'Kashmir Purple'
50cm by 45cm (20in by 18in)
Geranium x *magnificum*
60cm by 60cm (2ft by 2ft)
Helleborus x *hybridus* 'Pluto'
45cm by 45cm (18in by 18in)
Iris 'Black Swan'
75cm (2ft 6in)

Iris 'Langport Chapter'
   50cm (20in)
Iris 'Demon'
   30cm (1ft)
Limonium latifolium 'Violetta'
   60cm by 45cm (2ft by 18in)
Lupinus 'Storm'
   90cm by 75cm (3ft by 2ft 6in)
Phlox paniculata 'Blue Paradise'
   90cm by 70cm (3ft by 28in)
Thalictrum aquilegiifolium
'Thundercloud'
   90cm by 45cm (3ft by 18in)
Veronica spicata 'Romiley Purple'
   90cm by 30cm (3ft by 1ft)

SHRUBS

Lavandula angustifolia 'Hidcote'
   60cm by 75cm (2ft by 2ft 6in) (grey foliage)

BULBS

Dahlia 'Hillcrest Royal'
   1.1m by 60cm (3ft 6in by 2ft)

ANNUALS

Heliotropium arborescens 'Marine'
   45cm by 30cm (18in by 12in)

pale purples (lilac, mauve)

PERENNIALS

Geranium sylvaticum 'Mayflower'
   75cm by 60cm (2ft 6in by 2ft)
Hemerocallis 'Lilac Wine'
   40cm by 40cm (16in by 16in)
Nepeta 'Six Hills Giant'
   90cm by 60cm (3ft by 2ft)
Penstemon 'Alice Hindley'
   90cm by 45cm (3ft by 18in)
Penstemon 'Sour Grapes'
   60cm by 45cm (2ft by 18in)
Penstemon 'Stapleford Gem'
   60cm by 45cm (2ft by 18in)
Phlox paniculata 'Eventide'
   90cm by 60cm (3ft by 2ft)
Phlox paniculata 'Toits de Paris'
   90cm by 60cm (3ft by 2ft)
Salvia x superba 'Dear Anja'
   60cm by 45cm (2ft by 18in)

Thalictrum delavayi 'Hewitt's Double'
   1.2m by 60cm (4ft by 2ft)
Verbena bonariensis
   1.5m by 45cm (5ft by 18in)
Viola 'Inverurie Beauty'
   15cm by 20cm (6in by 8in)
Viola cornuta 'Boughton Blue'
   15cm by 15cm (6in by 6in)

SHRUBS

Rhododendron 'Blue Diamond'
   90cm by 1.2m (3ft by 4ft) (acid soil)
Rosa 'Bleu Magenta'
   3.5m by 3m (11ft by 10ft)
Syringa pubescens subsp. patula
'Miss Kim'
   2m by 1.5m (6ft by 5ft)

CLIMBERS

Wisteria floribunda 'Macrobotrys'

BULBS

Tulipa 'Bleu Aimable'
   55cm (22in)

oranges
intense orange (flame)

PERENNIALS

Achillea 'Forncett Fletton'
   75cm by 45cm (2ft 6in by 18in)
Crocosmia x crocosmiiflora 'Emily
McKenzie'
   60cm by 8cm (2ft by 3in)
Euphorbia griffithii 'Fireglow'
   75cm by 90m (2ft 6in by 3ft)
Geum 'Borisii'
   60cm to 30cm (2ft by 1ft)
Geum coccineum (syn. G. x borisii)
   50cm by 30cm (20in by 12in)
Helenium 'Sahin's Early Flowerer'
   75cm by 60cm (2ft 6in by 2ft)
Hemerocallis 'Mikado'
   90cm by 90cm (3ft by 3ft)
Iris spuria 'Imperial Bronze'
   90cm (3ft)
Iris 'Gingerbread Man'
   35cm (14in)
Kniphofia 'Bees' Sunset'
   90cm by 60cm (3ft by 2ft)

Leonotis leonurus
   2m by 1m (6ft by 3ft)
Pilosella aurantiaca (syn. Hieraceum
aurantiacum)
   20cm by 90cm (8in by 3ft)

SHRUBS

Berberis darwinii 'Flame'
   1.5 by 1.5m (5ft by 5ft)
Colutea x media
   3m by 3m (10ft by 10ft)
   (blue-green foliage)
Phygelius x rectus 'African Queen'
   90cm by 1.2m (3ft by 4ft)
Potentilla fruticosa 'Tangerine'
   90cm by 90cm (3ft by 3ft)
Rhododendron 'Spek's Brilliant'
(azalea)
   2.5m by 2.5m (8ft by 8ft) (acid soil)
Rosa 'Orange Sensation'
   70cm by 60cm (28in by 2ft)
Rosa Warm Welcome
   2m by 1.5m (6ft by 5ft)

CLIMBERS

Campsis x tagliabuana 'Madame
Galen'

BULBS

Alstroemeria aurea 'Dover Orange'
   80cm by 75cm (32in by 2ft 6in)
Fritillaria imperialis 'Aurora'
   1.5m (5ft)
Lilium 'African Queen'
   1.5–2m (5–6ft)
Lilium lancifolium var. splendens
(syn. L. tigrinum)
   60cm–1.5m (2–5ft) (acid soil)
Lilium superbum
   60–90cm (2–3ft) (acid soil)

pale oranges (apricot, peach)

PERENNIALS

Kniphofia 'Shining Sceptre'
   90cm by 60cm (3ft by 2ft)
Lupinus 'Amber Glow'
   45cm by 60cm (18in by 2ft)
Hemerocallis 'Michelle Coe'
   90cm by 75cm (3ft by 2ft 6in)

CLIMBERS

Rosa 'Meg'

BULBS

Tulipa 'Apricot Beauty'
  40cm (16in)

ANNUALS

Diascia barberae 'Hopley's Apricot'
  25cm by 25cm (10in by 10in)
Digitalis ferruginea 'Apricot Hybrids'
  90cm by 45cm (3ft by 18in)

dark oranges (copper, cinnamon, rust)

PERENNIALS

Achillea 'Walther Funcke'
  60cm by 45cm (2ft by 18in)
Chrysanthemum 'Bronze Elegance'
  90cm by 60cm (3ft by 2ft)
Helenium 'Coppelia'
  90cm by 60cm (3ft by 2ft)
Helenium 'Julisamt'
  90cm by 60cm (3ft by 2ft)
Helenium 'Moerheim Beauty'
  90cm by 60cm (3ft by 2ft)
Hemerocallis 'Mauna Loa'
  50cm by 90cm (20in by 3ft)
Iris 'Tuscan'
  90cm (3ft)
Kniphofia 'Cobra'
  90cm by 45cm (3ft by 18in)

ANNUALS

Helianthus 'Velvet Queen'
  1.5m by 60cm (5ft by 2ft)
Rudbeckia 'Chim Chiminee'
  60cm by 45cm (2ft by 18in)

greens
mid- and pale greens (grass, apple, jade, emerald)

PERENNIALS

Angelica archangelica
  2m by 1.2m (6ft by 4ft)

Aquilegia viridiflora
  30cm by 20cm (12in by 8in)
Astrantia major subsp. *involucrata* 'Shaggy'
  90cm by 60cm (3ft by 2ft)
Euphorbia polychroma
  40cm by 60cm (16in by 2ft)
Helleborus argutifolius (syn. *H. corsicus*)
  1.2m by 90cm (4ft by 3ft)
Helleborus foetidus
  80cm by 45cm (32in by 18in)
Heuchera 'Green Ivory'
  75cm by 75cm (2ft 6in by 2ft 6in)
Iris 'Cleo Murrell'
  90cm (3ft)
Iris 'Green Ice'
  85cm (32in)
Kniphofia 'Green Jade'
  1.5m by 60cm (5ft by 2ft)
Kniphofia 'Percy's Pride'
  1.2m by 60cm (4ft by 2ft)
Paris polyphylla
  90cm by 30cm (3ft by 12in)
Smyrnium perfoliatum
  80cm by 60cm (32in by 2ft)

SHRUBS

Bupleurum fruticosum
  2m by 2.5m (6ft by 8ft)
Euphorbia characias subsp. *wulfenii*
  1.2m by 1.2m (4ft by 4ft)
Itea ilicifolia
  5m by 3m (15ft by 10ft)
Stachyurus praecox
  4m by 3m (12ft by 10ft)

BULBS

Tulipa 'Spring Green'
  45cm (18in)

ANNUALS

Chenopodium botrys 'Green Magic'
  1.2m by 60cm (4ft by 2ft)
Molucella laevis
  90cm by 23cm (3ft by 9in)
Nicotiana langsdorfii
  1.5m by 35cm (5ft by 14in)
Nicotiana 'Lime Green'
  60cm by 25cm (2ft by 10in)

white

PERENNIALS

Anemone x *hybrida* 'Luise Uhink'
  1.2m by 60cm (4ft by 2ft)
Anemone x *hybrida* 'Whirlwind'
  1.2m by 60cm (4ft by 2ft)
Aquilegia vulgaris 'Nivea'
  90cm by 45cm (3ft by 18in)
Campanula persicifolia 'Hampstead White'
  90cm by 30cm (3ft by 1ft)
Dicentra spectabilis 'Alba'
  1.2m by 45cm (4ft by 18in)
Leucanthemum x *superbum* 'Phyllis Smith'
  90cm by 60cm (3ft by 2ft)
Leucanthemum x *superbum* 'Wirral Supreme'
  90cm by 75cm (3ft by 2ft 6in)
Papaver orientale 'Black and White'
  1.2m by 90cm (4ft by 3ft)
Phlox paniculata 'Fujiyama'
  75cm by 60cm (2ft 6in by 2ft)

SHRUBS

Anthemis cupaniana
  30cm by 50cm (12in by 20in)
  (silver foliage)
Chaenomeles speciosa 'Nivalis'
  2.5m by 5m (8ft by 15ft)
Chaenomeles x *superba* 'Jet Trail'
  1.5m by 2m (5ft by 6ft)
Choisya 'Aztec Pearl'
  2.5m by 2.5m (8ft by 8ft)
Cistus x *cyprius*
  1.5m by 1.5m (5ft by 5ft)
Escallonia 'Iveyi'
  3m by 3m (10ft by 10ft)
Hydrangea arborescens 'Annabelle'
  2.5m by 2.5m (8ft by 8ft)
Hydrangea quercifolia 'Snow Flake'
  2m by 2.5m (6ft by 8ft)
Myrtus communis 'Tarentina'
  1.5m by 1.5m (5ft by 5ft)
Romneya coulteri
  2.5m by 3m (8ft by 10ft) (grey foliage)
Syringa vulgaris 'Mme Lemoine'
  7m by 7m (22ft by 22ft)

CLIMBERS

Trachelospermum jasminoides
'Album'

BULBS

Lilium regale var. *album*
   1.5m (5ft)
Tulipa 'White Triumphator'
   75cm (2ft 6in)

other colours
browns (sepia, chestnut, bronze)

PERENNIALS

Chrysanthemum 'Brennpunkt'
   80cm by 45cm (32in by 18in)
Kniphofia 'Toffee Nosed'
   90cm by 60cm (3ft by 2ft)

SHRUBS

Rosa 'Edith Holden'
   1.5m by 1m (5ft by 3ft)

BULBS

Gladiolus 'Mileesh'
   1.7m by 15cm (5ft 6in by 6in)

'blacks' (extremely dark brown, deep purple, midnight-blue)

PERENNIALS

Aquilegia vulgaris var. *stellata*
'Black Barlow'
   90cm (3ft)
Delphinium 'Faust'
   2m by 75cm (6ft by 2ft 6in)
Iris 'Black Taffeta'
   80cm (32in)
Iris 'Midnight Oil'
   90cm (3ft)
Scabiosa 'Chile Black'
   45cm by 30cm (18in by 12in)

BULBS

Ranunculus asiaticus Turban Group
'Nearly Black'
   45cm by 20cm (18in by 8in)

ANNUALS

Alcea rosea 'Nigra'
   2m by 45cm (6ft by 18in)
Alcea rosea 'Jet Black'
   2m by 45cm (6ft by 18in)
Centaurea cyanus 'Black Ball'
   35cm by 25cm (14in by 10in)
Dianthus barbatus Nigrescens
Group 'Sooty' (biennial)
   45cm by 45cm (18in by 18in)
Ipomoea purpurea 'Kniolan's Black'
(climber)
Viola 'Blackjack'
   15cm by 15cm (6in by 6in)
Viola 'Molly Sanderson'
   15cm by 15cm (6in by 6in)
Viola tricolor 'Bowles' Black'
   10cm to 20cm (4in to 8in)
Viola x *wittrockiana* 'Black Moon'
   20cm by 30cm (8in by 12in)

mixed and muted

PERENNIALS

Digitalis ferruginea (buff, yellow,
brown)
   1.2m by 45cm (4ft by 18in)
Erysimum 'Jacob's Jacket' (bronze,
orange, lilac)
   30cm by 45cm (12in by 18in)
Iris 'Brown Lasso' (lavender, brown,
gold)
   90cm (3ft)
Iris 'Langport Duchess' (violet, coffee,
bronze, gold)
   40cm (16in)

ANNUALS

Lantana camara in var. (orange, pink,
yellow, cream)
   2m by 2m (6ft by 6ft)
Viola x *wittrockiana* Joker Series
(bi-colours and 'pansy faces' with
blue, mahogany, gold, violet)
   23cm by 30cm (9in by 12in)

foliage colour

greens
mid-greens (fresh, mint, apple, jade)

SHRUBS
Choisya ternata
  2.5m by 2.5m (8ft by 8ft)
Euphorbia characias subsp. *wulfenii* 'John Tomlinson'
  1.2m by 1.2m (4ft by 4ft)
Ficus carica 'Brown Turkey'
  3m by 4m (10ft by 12ft)
Griselinia littoralis
  8m by 5m (25ft by15ft)
Hebe albicans
  60cm by 90cm (2ft by 3ft)
Pittosporum tenuifolium 'Irene Paterson'
  1.2m by 60cm (4ft by 2ft)
Santolina chamaecyparissus 'Lemon Queen'
  60cm by 60cm (2ft by 2ft)

PERENNIALS
Foeniculum vulgare
  1.8m by 45cm (6ft by 18in)
Paris polyphylla (syn. *Diaswa polyphylla*)
  90cm by 30cm (3ft by 1ft)

dark green (bottle, olive)

SHRUBS
Aucuba japonica 'Rozannie'
  90cm by 1m (3ft by 3ft)
Osmanthus delavayi
  6m by 4m (20ft by 12ft)
Prunus laurocerasus 'Zabeliana'
  90cm (3ft) by 2.5m (8ft)
Prunus lusitanica
  20m by 20m (70ft by 70ft)
Pyracantha in var.
Taxus baccata (conifer)
  20m by 10m (70ft by 30ft)
Viburnum tinus 'Eve Price'
  5m by 4m (15ft by 12ft)

red and purple
(plum, wine, maroon)

SHRUBS
Berberis thunbergii 'Atropurpurea'
  2.5m by 2.5m (8ft by 8ft)
Cercis canadensis 'Forest Pansy'
  5m by 5m (15ft by 15ft)
Cotinus coggygria 'Royal Purple'
  5m by 5m (15ft by 15ft)
Weigela florida 'Foliis Purpureis'
  1m by 1.5m (3ft by 5ft)

TREES
Acer platanoides 'Crimson Sentry'
  12m by 5m (40ft by 15ft)
Cordyline australis 'Purple Tower'
  3–10m by 1–4m (10–30ft by 3–12ft)
Cordyline australis 'Torbay Red'
  3–10m by 1–4m (10–30ft by 3–12ft)
Gleditsia triacanthos 'Rubylace'
  15m by 10m (50ft by 30ft)
Prunus pissardii 'Nigra' (syn. *Prunus cerasifera* 'Pissardii')
  10m by 10m (30ft by 30ft)

PERENNIALS
Heuchera micrantha var. *diversifolia* 'Palace Purple'
(similar heucheras include 'Chocolate Ruffles', 'Black Velvet', 'Velvet Night', 'Purple Ace' 'Rachael', 'Harry Hay' and 'Can Can')
  45–60cm by 45–60cm (18in–2ft by 18in–2ft)
Lobelia 'Dark Crusader'
  90cm by 30cm (3ft by1ft) (damp soil)
Phormium tenax 'Purpureum'
  3m by 2m (10ft by 6ft)

BULBS
Dahlia 'Bishop of Llandaff'
  1.1m by 45cm (3ft 6in by 18in)
Dahlia 'David Howard'
  90cm by 50cm (3ft by 20in)

brown and 'black'
(bronze, chocolate, chestnut, ebony)

SHRUBS
Acer palmatum 'Chitosayama'
  2m by 3m (6ft by 10ft)
Corylus maxima 'Purpurea'
  7m by 5m (20ft by15ft)
Phormium tenax 'Bronze Baby'
  80cm by 80cm (32in by 32in)
Physocarpus opulifolius 'Diabolo'
  1.2m by 2m (4ft by 6ft)
Pittosporum tenuifolium 'Nigricans'
  3m by 1.5m (10ft by 5ft)
Ricinus communis 'Impala'
  1.2m by 1.2m (4ft by 4ft)
Sambucus nigra 'Black Beauty' (syn. 'Gerda')
  2m by 2m (6ft by 6ft)
Sambucus nigra 'Guincho Purple'
  2m by 2m (6ft by 6ft)
Viburnum sargentii 'Onondaga'
  2m by 2m (6ft by 6ft)

TREES
Fagus sylvatica 'Dawyck Purple'
  20m by 5m (70ft by 15ft)
Fagus sylvatica 'Purpurea Pendula'
  3m by 3m (10ft by 10ft)
Fagus sylvatica 'Riversii'
  25m by 15m (80ft by 50ft)

PERENNIALS
Cimicifuga simplex 'Brunette'
  1.2m by 60cm (4ft by 2ft)
Eupatorium rugosum 'Chocolate'
  1.8m by 60cm (6ft by 2ft)
Euphorbia dulcis 'Chameleon'
  30cm by 30cm (12in by 12in)
Foeniculum vulgare 'Purpureum'
  1.8m by 45cm (6ft by 18in)
Lychnis x *arkwrightii* 'Vesuvius'
  45cm by 30cm (18in by 12in)
Lysimachia ciliata 'Firecracker'
  1.2m by 60cm (4ft by 2ft)
Ophiopogon planiscapus 'Nigrescens'
  20cm by 30cm (8in by 12in)
Ranunculus ficaria 'Brazen Hussy'
  5cm by 30cm (2in by 12in)

GRASSES

Carex buchananii
60cm by 90cm (2ft by 3ft)

Carex comans 'Bronze Form'
35cm by 75cm (14in by 2ft 6in)

Carex flagellifera
1.1m by 90cm (3ft 6in by 3ft)

Carex petrei
25cm by 15cm (10in by 6in)

Uncinia rubra
30cm by 35cm (12in by 14in)

yellows
(gold, primrose, butter, lime)

SHRUBS

Philadelphus coronarius 'Aureus'
2.5m by 1.5m (8ft by 5ft)

Pittosporum tenuifolium
'Warnham Gold'
8m by 4m (25ft by 12ft)

Stachys byzantina 'Primrose Heron'
45cm by 60cm (18in by 2ft)

TREES

Gleditsia triacanthos 'Sunburst'
12m by 10m (40ft by 33ft)

PERENNIALS

Helichrysum 'Sulphur Light' (syn. H. 'Schwefellicht')
40cm (16in)

Hosta 'August Moon'
50cm by 75cm (20in by 2ft 6in)

Hosta 'Zounds'
55cm by 90cm (22in by 3ft)

GRASSES

Luzula sylvatica 'Aurea'
70cm by 45cm (28in by 18in)

Milium effusum 'Aureum'
60cm by 30cm (2ft by 1ft)

silver and grey

SHRUBS

Convolvulus cneorum
60cm by 90cm (2ft by 3ft)

Elaeagnus angustifolia 'Quicksilver'
4m by 4m (12ft by 12ft)

Hebe 'Pewter Dome'
40cm by 60cm (16in by 2ft)

Hebe pimeleoides 'Quicksilver'
45cm by 60cm (18in by 2ft)

Lavandula angustifolia 'Hidcote'
60cm by 75cm (2ft by 2ft 6in)

Santolina chamaecyparissus
50cm by 1m (20in by 3ft)

Stachys byzantina 'Silver Carpet'
45cm by 60cm (18in by 2ft)

TREES

Pyrus salicifolia 'Pendula'
5m by 4m (15ft by 12ft)

PERENNIALS

Anthemis punctata subsp. cupaniana
30cm by 90cm (1ft by 3ft)

Artemisia 'Powis Castle'
60cm by 90cm (2ft by 3ft)

Artemisia alba 'Canescens'
45cm by 30cm (18in by 12in)

Artemisia ludoviciana 'Valerie Finnis'
60cm by 60cm (2ft by 2ft)

Artemisia schmidtiana 'Nana'
30cm by 45cm (12in by 18in)

Heuchera 'Pewter Moon'
40cm by 30cm (16in by 12in)

Macleaya cordata
2.5m by 1m (8ft by 3ft)

Melianthus major
3m by 3m (10ft by 10ft)

GRASSES

Elymus hispidus
75cm by 40cm (2ft 6in by 16in)

blues

SHRUBS

Brahea armata
15m by 7m (50ft by 22ft)
(frost-tender palm)

Ruta graveolens 'Jackman's Blue'
60cm by 75cm (2ft by 2ft 6in)

PERENNIALS

Eryngium amethystinum
70cm by 70cm (28in by 28in)

Eryngium x oliverianum
90cm by 45cm (3ft by 18in)

Hosta 'Blue Angel'
1m by 1.2m (3ft by 4ft)

Hosta 'Halcyon'
40cm by 70cm (16in by 28in)

GRASSES

Elymus magellanicus
15cm by 30cm (6in by 12in)

Festuca glauca 'Elijah Blue'
30cm by 25cm (1ft by 10in)

Helictotrichon sempervirens (syn. Avena candida)
1.4m by 60cm (4ft 6in by 2ft)

Leymus arenarius
1.5m (5ft) spreading

variegated
(white and yellow variegation)

SHRUBS

Cornus alba 'Elegantissima'
3m by 3m (10ft by 10ft)

Cornus alba 'Spaethii'
3m by 3m (10ft by 10ft)

Euonymus fortunei 'Emerald Gaiety'
90cm by 1.5m (3ft by 5ft)

Philadelphus coronarius 'Variegatus'
2.5m by 2m (8ft by 6ft)

Phormium 'Sundowner'
2m by 2m (6ft by 6ft)

Weigela florida 'Variegata'
2.5m by 2.5m (8ft by 8ft)

PERENNIALS

Astrantia major 'Sunningdale Variegated'
90cm by 45cm (3ft by 18in)

Iris pallida 'Argentea Variegata'
1.2m (4ft)

Ophiopogon jaburan 'Vittatus'
60cm by 30cm (2ft by 1ft)

Sisyrinchium striatum 'Aunt May'
50cm by 25cm (20in by 10in)

index

acknowledgments

author's acknowledgments

The Quadrille team has, as always, been thorough, caring and professional and I would like to thank them and the RHS for giving me the opportunity to write this book. Jane O'Shea, who commissioned it, followed its progress with constant interest and encouragement. Francoise Dietrich has once again produced a book that is designed with originality and flair, while Lynne Robinson and Richard Lowther have interpreted my planting schemes with stylish paintings that express the pleasures and the effectiveness of colour. Marianne Majerus scoured gardens to produce superb quality photographs sensitive to the nuances of colour. Finally, I must say how very much I value the continuous considered editing of Carole McGlynn. She responds to each new subject with enthusiasm and helped me greatly with her clarity of thought when I became mired in the subject matter.

photographic acknowledgments

1 Nicola Browne/Piet Oudolf; 2-3 Andrew Lawson/ Sticky Wicket, Dorchester, Dorset; 4-5 Marianne Majerus; 6-7 Marianne Majerus/RHS Wisley; 9 Jill Billington/ Design: Tom Hobbs, Vancouver; 10-11 Marianne Majerus; 12-13 Carol Fulton; 14 Jill Billington/Mrs Marnie McNeill, Victoria, British Columbia, Canada; 15 Marianne Majerus/Design: Tom Stuart-Smith; 18 above Gary Rogers; 18 below Marianne Majerus/RHS Wisley; 19 left S & O Mathews/The White House Sussex; 19 centre Nicola Browne; 19 right Marianne Majerus/Cherry Tree Lodge Nursery, Lancs; 20 S & O Mathews/Design: Phillippa Lambert; 21 above S & O Mathews/The Little Cottage, Hampshire; 21 below Marcus Harpur; 22 left Jerry Harpur; 22 right Marianne Majerus/Charney Well, Cumbria; 23 above Marianne Majerus/Cherry Tree Lodge Nursery, Lancs; 23 below Marianne Majerus; 24 Jerry Harpur/Design:Ian Pollard, Wiltshire; 25 Marianne Majerus/Clos Normand; 26-7 Marianne Majerus/Weir House, Design: Jill Billington & Barbara Hunt; 27 S & O Mathews/RHS Wisley; 28 above Marianne Majerus/RHS Rosemoor; 28 centre above Marianne Majerus/RHS Rosemoor; 28 centre below Marianne Majerus/RHS Chelsea; 28 below Marianne Majerus 29 above left Marianne Majerus/Hadspen House, Somerset, Design: Nori & Sandra Pope; 29 above right Marianne Majerus; 29 above centre left Marianne Majerus; 29above centre right Marianne Majerus/RHS Wisley; 29 below centre left Marianne Majerus/RHS Rosemoor; 29 below centre right Marianne Majerus/ Westonbirt Arboretum; 29 below left Marianne Majerus; 29 below right Marianne Majerus/ The Garden House, Buckland Monachorum; 30-1 Marianne Majerus/Glen Chantry, Essex; 32-3 Marianne Majerus;

33 S & O Mathews/Merrie Cottage, Hampshire; 34 Andrew Lawson; 35 Marianne Majerus/ RHS Wisley; 36 Jerry Harpur/RHS Chelsea 1998, Design Sarah Raven; 37 Marianne Majerus/The Garden House, Buckland Monachorum; 38-9 Marianne Majerus; 40-1 Mariyke Heuff/Design: Ton ter Linden; 42-3 Marianne Majerus/Design: Tessa Hobbs; 44 Marianne Majerus/ Design:Lee Heyhoop; 45 Marianne Majerus/The Garden House, Buckland Monachorum; 46 Marianne Majerus/Hadspen House, Somerset, Design: Nori & Sandra Pope; 49 Andrew Lawson/ Hampton Court Flower Show 2000, Design: Land Art; 50-1 Marianne Majerus/Hampton Court Flower Show 2001; 51 Christian Sarramon 52 S & O Mathews/RHS Wisley; 53 Marianne Majerus/Glen Chantry,Essex; 54 Marianne Majerus/Lady Farm,Glos; 57 left Nicola Browne/ Design: Bosvigo; 57 right Marianne Majerus/ Bourton House,Glos; 58-9 Marianne Majerus; 59 Marianne Majerus; 60 Marianne Majerus/Coton Manor, Northants; 61 left Andrew Lawson/RHS Chelsea 2000, Design: Piet Oudolf & Arne Maynard; 61 right Marianne Majerus; 62 Marianne Majerus; 63 Andrew Lawson/ Sticky Wicket, Dorchester, Dorset; 64-5 Marianne Majerus/The Old Vicarage, East Ruston; 66-7 Marianne Majerus/RHS Wisley; 67 Marianne Majerus; 68 left Marianne Majerus/The Garden House, Buckland Monachorum; 68 right Jonathan Buckley/Glen Chantry, Essex, Design: Sue & Wol Staines; 69 Marianne Majerus/Vann, Surrey; 70 Marianne Majerus; 73 above Anthony Lord/The Manor House, Heslington; 73 below S & 0 Mathews/RHS Wisley; 74-5 Marianne Majerus; 76 Marianne Majerus; 77 Gary Rogers 79 above Jerry Harpur/Annie Wilkes, Sydney, Australia; 79 below Clive Nichols/RHS Chelsea 2000, Design: Piet Oudolf & Arne Maynard; 80 above Marianne Majerus; 80 below Marianne Majerus; 80 S & O Mathews/Broadhatch House, Hampshire; 82-3 Nicola Browne/Design: Piet Oudolf; 84-5 Jerry Harpur/Design: Penelope Hobhouse, Spain; 86-7 Anthony Lord/Great Dixter; 88 left Jerry Harpur/ Wollerton Old Hall, Shropshire; 88-9 John Glover/RHS Wisley, Design: Penelope Hobhouse; 90 above Anthony Lord; 90 below Jill Billington/ Chaumont 2001; 92 Marianne Majerus/Trewithen, Cornwall; 93 left Nicola Browne/Design: Dan Pearson; 93 right Jerry Harpur/Chateau Pontrancart, France; 94 left John Glover/Sticky Wicket, Dorset; 94 right Andrew Lawson; 95 Nicola Browne/The Garden House, Buckland Monachorum, Devon; 96 Marianne Majerus/Design: Beth Chatto; 96-7 Nicola Browne/Design: Dan Pearson; 97 Nicola Browne/Design: Piet Oudolf; 98-9 Georgia Glynn-Smith/Garden Picture Library; 99 Marianne Majerus/The Garden House, Buckland Monachorum, Devon; 100 Marianne Majerus/Wretham Lodge, Norfolk; 101 Marianne Majerus/RHS Rosemoor; 103 Jerry Harpur/Design: Beth Chatto; 104 Marianne Majerus/Desgin: Lee Heykoop; 105 Marianne Majerus/ Hadspen Garden, Somerset, Design: Nori & Sandra Pope; 106 Marianne Majerus/RHS Rosemoor; 107 Clive Nichols/Mr Poulton, Swinton Lane, Worcs; 108 Marianne Majerus/ Cartier Garden, RHS Chelsea

2000, Design: Mark Anthony Walker; 109 Jerry Harpur/Ian Pollard; 110-11 Marianne Majerus/The Garden House, Buckland Monachorum, Devon; 112 Marianne Majerus; 113 above Marianne Majerus; 113 below Nicola Browne/Design: Dan Pearson; 114 above Andrew Lawson/Hampton Court Flower Show; 114 below S & O Mathews/RHS Wisley; 116 Marianne Majerus; 117 Nicola Browne/Design: Piet Oudolf; 118 Andrew Lawson; 120 Marianne Majerus; 122 above Jill Billington/Il Biviere Lentini, Sicily; 122 below Jerry Harpur/Great Dixter, East Sussex; 124 Marianne Majerus/The Garden House, Buckland Monachorum, Devon; 126-7 Marianne Majerus/Design: George Carter; 128-9 Marianne Majerus/Levens Hall, Cumbria; 130 Marianne Majerus/Elton Hall, Herefordshire; 131 Marianne Majerus/ Glen Chantry, Essex; 133 above Marianne Majerus; 133 below Marianne Majerus/RHS Rosemoor; 134 above Marianne Majerus/RHS Wisley; 134 below Marianne Majerus/Glen Chantry, Essex; 135 below Marianne Majerus/Glen Chantry, Essex; 135 Marianne Majerus/Benington Lordship; 136 Marianne Majerus; 136-7 Marianne Majerus/Design: Tom Stuart-Smith; 139 above Marianne Majerus/Grafton Cottage, Staffs; 139 below Marianne Majerus/Charney Well, Cumbria; 141 above Marianne Majerus/The Cartier Garden, RHS Chelsea 2000, Design: Mark Anthony; 141 below Marianne Majerus Grafton Cottage Staffs; 142 Marianne Majerus/RHS Wisley; 142-3 Marianne Majerus; 144 Marianne Majerus/RHS Chelsea 2001, Design: Norwood Hall ETC; 145 Marianne Majerus/ Design: Jill Billington; 146 above Marianne Majerus; 146 centre Marianne Majerus/Design: George Carter; 146 below Marianne Majerus/Pots & Pithoi; 148-9 Marianne Majerus; 150-1 Marianne Majerus/ Hadspen Garden, Somerset, Design: Nori & Sandra Hope; 152 above Marianne Majerus; 152 below Marianne Majerus/Design: Tom Stuart-Smith; 153 left Marianne Majerus/The Garden of the Elements, RHS Chelsea 2001; 153 centre Marianne Majerus/Design: Mark Brown; 153 right Marianne Majerus/Turn End, Bucks, Design: Peter Aldington; 155 Marianne Majerus; 156 Marcus Harpur/Dr Mary Giblin, Essex; 157 Marianne Majerus/ Design: Lee Heykoop; 158-9 Marianne Majerus Great Comp, Kent; 160 Marianne Majerus; 161 Jerry Harpur/Design: Beth Chatto; 162 above Marianne Majerus/Saling Hall, Essex; 162 below Marianne Majerus/ Westonbirt, Aboretum, Glos; 164-5 Christian Sarramon; 167 above Marianne Majerus; 167 below Marianne Majerus; 168 Marianne Majerus/The Old Vicarage, East Rushton, Norfolk; 169 Andrew Lawson/Tresco, Isles of Scilly; 170 Marianne Majerus; 170-1 Peter Anderson/Tuscan Arizona, USA; 172 above Marianne Majerus/The Old Vicarage, East Rushton, Norfolk; 172 below Marianne Majerus/ Beeston Hall, Norfolk; 174 above Marianne Majerus/ RHS Wisley; 174 below Marianne Majerus/RHS Rosemoor; 175 Marianne Majerus; 176 Clay Perry.